Table of Contents

1   Introducing Dreamweaver   7

What is Dreamweaver?	8
Obtaining Dreamweaver	9
Installing Dreamweaver	10
First view	11
Preferences	12
Panels	12
Objects palette	13
Status Bar	13
Objects palette	14
Properties Inspector	19
Launcher palette	21
External editors	24
Page properties	26
Menus and the toolbar	27
Getting help	28
Dreamweaver Help	28
O'Reilly Reference	28

2   Setting up a site   29

Planning a site	30
Preparing a structure	30
Creating a new site	31
Adding pages	32
Saving files	34
Opening files	35
Switching between windows	36
Switching to the site window	36
Switching to Design view	36
Setting a home page	37
Viewing the site map	39
Defining a site	40

3   HTML in Dreamweaver   41

HTML overview	42
Common tags	43
Page views	44
HTML preferences	45
Code colours	45
Code format	47
Roundtrip HTML	48
Rewriting preferences	50
Invalid code	51
Cleaning up HTML	52

Cleaning up Word HTML 53
Quick Tag editor 54
Quick Tag preferences 57
Selecting and removing tags 58

4 Assets 59

Managing assets 60
   Creating Favorites 61
   Applying assets 61
Using templates 62
Creating templates 63
Editing templates 65
Creating editable regions 66
Template properties 67
Creating pages from templates 69
Updating pages based on templates 70
About the Library 71
Creating Library items 72
Adding items from the Library 73
Editing Library items 74
Creating editable navigation bars 76

5 Adding text 77

Inserting text 78
Text properties 79
Fonts 80
   Adding more fonts 81
Size 82
Colour 84
Emphasis and alignment 85
Lists 86
Indents 87
Copy and Paste 88
   Basic Copy and Paste 88
   Using Paste as HTML 88

6 Working with images 89

Web image overview 90
Using images effectively 91
Inserting images 92
Image properties 93
Resizing images 94
Aligning images and text 95
   Alignment buttons 96
Creating rollover images 97

7 Using hyperlinks 99

About hyperlinks 100
Document-relative links 101
Absolute links 102
Email links 102
Linking to documents 103
Linking to anchors 105
Creating an email link 107
Point-to-file links 108
Image maps 111
Navigation bars 112

8 Tables and Layout view 113

Designing with tables 114
Inserting a table 115
Editing a table 117
Adding and deleting rows and columns 119
Selecting cells 120
Adding content 122
Adding text 122
Adding images and more 122
Aligning items in a table 123
Creating nested tables 124
Layout view 125

9 Frames and layers 129

About frames 130
Creating frames 131
Frames from new documents 131
Using preset designs 132
Converting existing documents into frames 132
Saving frames and framesets 133
Frames Inspector 135
Frame/frameset properties 136
Resizing and deleting frames 138
Hyperlinks in frames 139
Targeting links 140
Using layers 143
Creating layers 144
Layer properties 145
Layers palette 146
Creating nested layers 147
Moving and resizing layers 148

Forms   149

10

Uses for forms	150
Creating forms	151
Inserting text fields	152
Inserting checkboxes	153
Inserting radio buttons	154
Inserting file fields	155
Inserting lists/menus	156
Menu properties	156
List properties	156
Adding list/menu items	157
Inserting hidden fields	158
Inserting jump menus	159
Inserting buttons	160

Advanced features   161

11

HTML styles	162
Cascading Style Sheets styles	164
Creating CSS style sheets	165
Applying CSS style sheets	167
Animation	168
Modifying animation paths	170
Flash buttons and text	171
Behaviors	172
Javascript	174

Publishing   175

12

Site window preferences	176
Site management	177
Using the site map	178
Uploading a site	180
Getting and putting files	183
Checking files in and out	184
Synchronising files	186

Index   187

Introducing Dreamweaver

Dreamweaver is a powerful Web authoring tool that can be used to create highly professional-looking sites. This chapter looks at obtaining and installing the program and explains some of the features that will enable you to start working at creating Web pages.

Covers

What is Dreamweaver? | 8

Obtaining Dreamweaver | 9

Installing Dreamweaver | 10

First view | 11

Preferences | 12

Objects palette | 14

Properties Inspector | 19

Launcher palette | 21

External editors | 24

Page properties | 26

Menus and the toolbar | 27

Getting help | 28

Chapter One

What is Dreamweaver?

Before you start creating Web pages, it is a good idea to learn the basics of HTML, either with a book or a course. There are numerous training courses and night-classes in HTML coding.

In the early days of Web design, the code used to create Web pages was input manually. This required the page designers to have a reasonable amount of knowledge of this code, HyperText Markup Language (HTML). While this is not a full-blown computer language and it can be learnt reasonably quickly, it can be a time-consuming business to create complicated Web pages in this fashion.

The next development in Web design software was the introduction of HTML editors. These are programs that help make the process of creating HTML quicker and easier by giving the author shortcuts for adding the elements that make up the coded page. However, this still requires a good basic knowledge of HTML: it makes the process quicker for the experienced designer but it does not help the novice much.

Even when you are using a WYSIWYG Web authoring program, it is still important to follow the basics of good Web design. For an excellent introduction to this, take a look at 'Web Page Design in easy steps'.

The big breakthrough in Web design software, and one that introduced a huge new audience to the joys of Web design, was the introduction of WYSIWYG programs. This stands for What You See Is What You Get and they enable people to design their own Web pages without having to even be aware of the existence of HTML. They work in a similar way to a word processing or a desktop publishing program: what you layout on the screen is what the end user will see on their computer. With these programs, the HTML is still present (and you can edit it manually if you desire) but it is all generated automatically by the program in the background.

Dreamweaver is a WYSIWYG Web authoring program that provides an effective interface for quickly creating high quality Web pages. In addition, it contains a range of powerful tools for incorporating the latest Web design elements into sites to give them a highly professional look. Overall, Dreamweaver is an ideal program for anyone involved in designing Web sites: its combination of simplicity and power makes it an excellent choice for the novice and professional alike.

Obtaining Dreamweaver

With their range of Web authoring and multimedia products, Macromedia can provide everything you need to create truly cutting edge Web sites.

Dreamweaver is produced by Macromedia, one of the market leaders in Web design software. They produce a wide range of products for incorporating the latest Web design technology, including programs such as Flash and Fireworks, and Dreamweaver allows easy integration with other Macromedia products, to provide the greatest power and flexibility for the least amount of effort.

Dreamweaver can be obtained from most good software suppliers, although in some cases it may have to be ordered. Alternatively it can be downloaded directly from the Dreamweaver page on the Macromedia site:

If you want to purchase the retail version of Dreamweaver while you are using the 30-day trial version, click on the Buy Now button on the program's startup window.

- www.macromedia.com/software/dreamweaver/

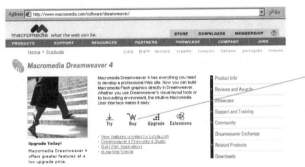

On the Dreamweaver page, click Buy to begin downloading the program

For image editing, Dreamweaver is very closely integrated with Fireworks. There is not space to deal with this in this book but if you want to know more, take at look at my book 'Fireworks in easy steps'.

If you want to try out Dreamweaver before you buy it, a 30-day trial version can also be downloaded from the following Macromedia site:

- www.macromedia.com/software/dreamweaver/trial

This is a fully functioning version of the program and it allows you to purchase the retail version at any time during the trial period.

Trial versions of other Macromedia products, such as Flash and Fireworks, can also be downloaded from their Web site.

Installing Dreamweaver

Windows needs the following minimum system requirements if you want to run Dreamweaver 4:

- *Pentium Processor (Pentium II recommended)*
- *Windows 95, 98, Me, 2000 or NT 4 (with Service Pack)*
- *64 Mb of RAM*
- *150 Mb of available disc space*
- *800 x 600 256 colour monitor*
- *CD-ROM drive*

For installation on a Mac:

- *Power Macintosh Processor (G3 or higher recommended)*
- *Mac OS8.6 or above*
- *64 Mb of RAM*
- *150 Mb of disc space*
- *800 x 600 256 colour monitor*
- *Adobe Type Manager 4*
- *CD-ROM drive*

Before installing Dreamweaver, either by downloading it from the Macromedia site or from a retail CD-ROM, it is necessary to ensure that your computer is capable of running the program to its full capacity. Due to some of the multimedia elements that can be incorporated into Dreamweaver it is important that the requirements on the left are met, otherwise you may encounter problems when trying to utilise certain parts of the program.

When you begin to install Dreamweaver, either by downloading it or from a CD-ROM, a screen will appear informing you that the installation process is about to begin. Select Next to continue through the steps of the installation process. This will include the automatic creation of a folder into which all of the Dreamweaver files will be placed. Unless you have a good reason not to, leave this default folder as the one chosen by the program.

Once the installation process has been completed, the best way to access Dreamweaver is to place a shortcut (PC) or alias (Mac) on your desktop. To create a desktop shortcut on a PC, locate the program in its application folder, right-click on it and drag it onto the desktop. Release the icon and select Create Shortcut(s) Here from the menu. To create a desktop shortcut on a Mac, select the item, then select File>Make Alias from the menu bar. Once the alias has been created, you can move it to where you want it. The following icon should then be visible on the desktop. Double-click it to launch the program:

Dreamweaver can also be purchased as a studio package with Fireworks. This means that the two programs come together on the same CD-ROM. This is cheaper than buying the two programs separately.

If you have created a shortcut or alias on your desktop, double-click on this icon to launch Dreamweaver

First view

When you first launch Dreamweaver you should see the screen below. The main difference between the Dreamweaver interface and many other software programs is its extensive use of floating palettes. These are palettes containing the tools used by Dreamweaver, and they can be dragged and placed anywhere on the screen. Because of this, a toolbar does not automatically appear at the top of the screen underneath the menu bar, as you might expect. There are numerous palettes that can be used in Dreamweaver and the three most commonly used are displayed when the program is first opened:

When you first open Dreamweaver, there may be other palettes visible, such as the History palette. At this point, they are not required and they can be closed down as you would normally close a window on a PC or a Mac.

Toolbar   Menu bar   Objects palette. This enables you to insert a variety of objects in pages

Design view. This is where the content of new pages is created

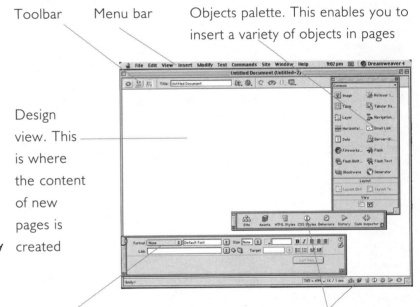

The palettes can be dragged around the screen and repositioned, depending on how you like to have your screen organised, or what you are working on at the time. When you are creating pages, you will probably move the palettes several times.

Properties Inspector. This displays the properties of the currently selected item on the page i.e. if a piece of text is selected then its properties would be displayed and if a graphic were selected then the image properties would be shown

Launcher palette. This contains shortcuts to other palettes within the program. A minimised version is also available at the bottom of the screen

Preferences

Dreamweaver offers extensive options for the way the program looks and operates. These are located in the Preferences menu:

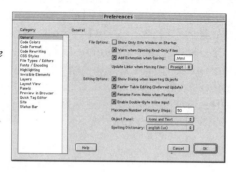

Take some time to look at the available preferences in Dreamweaver. Although you will not use all of them at this point, it is a good way to get a feel for the types of things that you can change within the program.

The preferences can be used to change the way the program and its elements appear, and also to change the way certain tasks are performed. There are dozens of these preferences, which cover specific elements of the program, and these will be covered in the relevant chapters to which they apply. However, there are some preferences that are useful to look at before you start using Dreamweaver.

Panels

These preferences can be used to select which palette you want to have displayed and which items you want included in the Launcher palette.

Try not to have too many palettes displayed at the one time. This causes the screen to become cluttered and it will make it harder to work on the content for your pages.

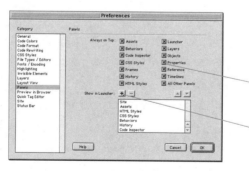

Open the Preferences window. Click here to show or hide palettes, and click here to add items to the Launcher palette

Objects palette

This option is contained within the General preference options and can be used to determine how the information in the Objects palette is displayed. Since this is one of the most commonly used palettes, it is worthwhile having it set up the way that you want:

If the Objects palette is displayed with icons and text it takes up more room on screen. However, this should be offset against the fact that it can be quicker to locate items within the palette.

Click here to select whether the items in the Objects palette are displayed as icons, text or both

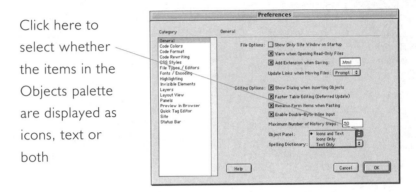

Status Bar

This determines the options for the Status Bar that is located at the bottom right of the program. This displays information about the size of the currently active file, how long it will take to download at the current modem setting, the size it will be displayed and whether a mini version of the Launcher is displayed:

The Status Bar has an option for testing how long a page will take to download over the Internet at a particular modem speed. This is a good way to see how long graphics and multimedia elements will take to download. Always test pages at the lowest modem speed first, since if it is acceptable at this level then there should not be any problem for other users. If a page takes longer than 20–30 seconds to download then think about editing some of the items it contains.

Check this box on to display the mini version of the Launcher in the Status Bar

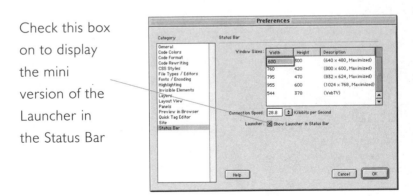

Objects palette

The Objects palette is a powerful and versatile tool for adding content to a Web page. It has six separate panels, which can be accessed from the Objects palette menu:

Keep the Objects palette visible on screen at all times, since you will use the elements within it throughout the Web authoring process.

Click here to access the Objects palette menu. Click on an option to display the elements which it contains

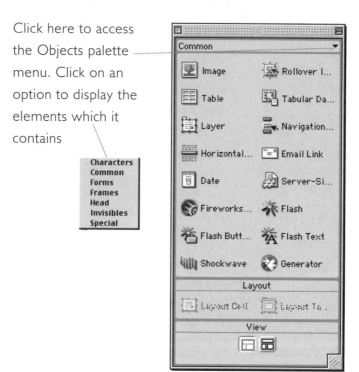

Common

This is the default setting and the one that contains some of the most commonly used elements on a Web page:

Tables do not just have to be used for numerical data — they are an excellent option for formatting text and graphics and they can be used to create complex designs.

- Image. This enables you to insert GIF or JPEG images into a page

- Rollover Image. This provides an option for creating a rollover image i.e. one that changes from one image to another when the cursor is moved over it. To do this, you have to select the images that you want to use to create the rollover effect

- Table. This enables you to insert a table and specify its initial properties

Use the horizontal rule option to insert lines to divide items on a page. This can include separating images, text and tables.

If you intend to use navigation bars on your Web sites, plan the structure of your sites carefully before you create your navigation bar. Otherwise you may find that you have missed out some pages and so you will have to redo or edit your navigation bar.

Fireworks is a Macromedia program designed specifically for creating and editing images for the Web.

Flash is a Macromedia program for creating animated effects and interactive elements on a Web page. If it is used carefully it can have a dramatic effect on a Web site.

- Tabular Data. This can be used to import data that has been created in the form of a spreadsheet table in another program. Dreamweaver can then recreate it in the same format as the original

- Layer. This is a Dreamweaver device that provides the facility for creating layers within a publication. This means that several layers of content can be placed on top of one another

- Navigation Bar. This enables you to create and insert a navigation bar. This can then be used to move around the pages on your site. If necessary, the navigation bar can be included on all pages within a site

- Horizontal Rule. This inserts a horizontal line directly below the current position of the cursor

- E-Mail Link. This can be used to create a link that allows the user to send an email to a predefined address

- Date. This inserts the current date at the insertion point

- Server-Side include. This can be used to tell the server that is hosting your Web site to include a particular file

- Fireworks . This enables you to insert images that have been created in Fireworks

- Flash. This enables you to insert a Flash movie

- Flash Button. This is a new device in Dreamweaver, that lets you create animated buttons

- Flash Text. This is another new element, that lets you create animated text

- Shockwave. This enables you to insert a Shockwave movie

- Generator. This enables you to insert a Generator document

Characters

This panel contains options for inserting special characters such as Copyright and Trademark.

Forms

This panel contains all of the elements that are required to create a form on a Web page:

If you are using trade names or brand names on your sites, it is best to include the relevant trademarks symbols.

- Form. This inserts the form holder boundary. It acts as a container into which the elements of the form are inserted

- Text Field. This inserts a text field which can then have its properties set

- Button. This inserts a Submit or Reset button

If you are using forms, you will have to make sure that your Internet Service Provider (ISP) has the facility for processing them. This usually involves a piece of programming script that can analyse the information that is sent from the form and then return it to you in a suitable format.

- Checkbox. This inserts boxes from which several options can be selected

- Radio Button. This inserts buttons that enable the user to select one option from a list, such as a Yes or No question

- List/Menu. This inserts a drop-down list or menu, to which numerous options can be added

- File Field. This inserts a file field which can be used to enable the user to insert files from their own hard drives

- Image Field. This can be used to insert a specific image rather than the generic Submit and Reset buttons

- Hidden Field. This inserts a hidden field that can then be used to gather information about the person using the form

- Jump Menu. This enables you to insert a menu to which links to other files can be included

Frames are a useful device if you want to retain an index on screen while the user can change the content of other parts of the page.

Frames can cause problems for search engines on the Web and in some cases they will not be able to identify your site. If in doubt, do not use frames on your home page.

One alternative to using frames for an index, is to use navigation bars instead.

Although the Head information does not directly affect the content on your page, it is important to include it for when your site is published on the Web. Not only will it help search engines find and index your site, it will also show other Web designers that you take a professional approach, if they choose to look at your source code.

Frames

This panel contains options for creating different styles of framesets. A frameset can be described as a collection of different pages that appear as a single page on a Web site. The selected style of the frameset determines the layout of the individual pages:

- Left, Right, Top and Bottom. These all create initial framesets that contain areas for two pages to be displayed. The page is split according to the selection. Once a page has been split this way, it can then also be sub-divided further by selecting another option

- Left and Top, Left Top, Top Left, Split. This enables you to create more complex framesets by allowing multiple pages to be displayed within them

Head

This panel contains information that is included in the header information of a Web page. This is not displayed in the main work area of Dreamweaver, but it can be viewed by looking at the source HTML code. The type of information is used to identify its content and also include keywords:

- Meta. This can be used to record information about the current page and also send information to the server hosting the page

- Keywords. This enables you to insert keywords that can be used by search engines on the Web

- Description. This can be used to write a short description of your page. This is also used by search engines, so keep it concise and relevant

- Refresh. This enables you to enter information about how long to wait before your page is automatically reloaded over the Web

- Base. This is the base URL related to the current page

- Link. This defines the relationship between the current file and another document

Invisibles

This panel displays elements on the page that give information about the current page but are not shown when the page is published on the Web. It is possible to hide or show all of the Invisibles on a page:

If the Invisibles are displayed in Dreamweaver they are shown as small yellow icons relating to the relevant Invisible. For some Invisibles, such as Comment, you can click on the icon to access its functionality.

Select View>Visual Aids> Invisible Elements from the menu bar

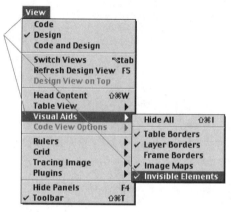

In previous versions of Dreamweaver, the Invisible panel contained an icon for inserting a non-breaking space. To do this in Dreamweaver 4, select Insert>Special Characters>Non-Breaking Space from the Menu bar.

This menu can also be used to insert a line break, which appeared on the Common Objects palette in previous versions. Another way to do this is by holding down Shift and pressing Return.

The items contained in the Invisibles palette are:

• Named Anchor. This enables you to link to another item on the same page, which can be useful if you want the user to be able to navigate around a long page. The Named Anchor invisible denotes the presence of an anchor on the page

• Comment. This gives you the option to add comments about your page at specific points, such as the need to include an image at a later date. This can be particularly useful if you are designing a Web site as part of a team

• Script. This enables you to write your own piece of script, such as JavaScript or VB Script and the invisible denotes its presence on the page

Properties Inspector

The Properties palette displays the attributes of the currently selected item on the page, whether it is an image, a piece of text, a table or a frame. In addition to viewing these attributes, they can also be altered by entering values within the Properties palette. For instance, if you want to change the size of an image, you can select it and then enter the new size that is required. To display the properties of a certain element it has to be selected first.

Image properties

Select an image by clicking on it once to display its relevant Properties palette:

Size   Dimensions   Location   Link   Alignment

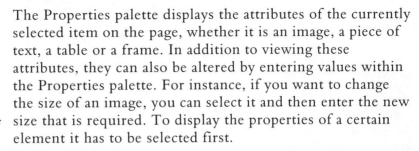

Text properties

Select a paragraph of text by inserting the cursor anywhere within it, or select specific pieces of text by clicking and dragging the cursor over them:

Style   Font   Size   Colour   Bold/Italic

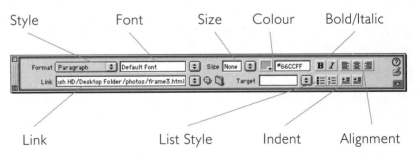

Link   List Style   Indent   Alignment

Table properties

Select a table by clicking once on its bottom border. This will display the properties for the table itself, not the content inside it:

The size of a table's rows and columns can be altered by clicking and dragging on their borders. For more information on tables, see Chapter Eight.

Number or Rows and Columns   Width and Height   Cell Padding and Spacing

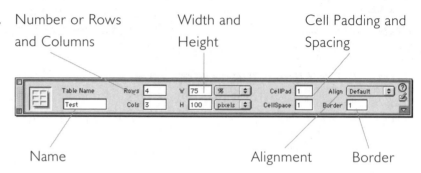

Name   Alignment   Border

Frame properties

If you are working with a frameset layout, its properties can be displayed by clicking once on one of the frame borders within the frameset:

A frameset is a page that consists of different frames. Framesets can be made up of a minimum of two individual frames, or they can consist of dozens. If there are numerous frames on a page this can make the design process more complicated. For more information on frames and framesets, see Chapter Nine.

Rows and Columns   Border   Border Colour

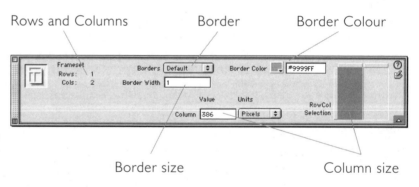

Border size   Column size

Launcher palette

The Launcher palette provides quick access to other elements of Dreamweaver. It can be customised to display different items to the default ones, as shown on page 13. The elements within the Launcher can be accessed by clicking on them once:

Site

This brings up a window that displays the structure of the current site:

The Site window shows you all of the files that are in the current site and how they interrelate (link) with each other. For more information on site structure, see Chapter Two.

Assets

This brings up a window that can be used to store items that you want to reuse throughout your Web site. This could include images, hyperlinks, Flash items, colours, scripts or library items:

Library items are either images or text that can be stored and used throughout a Web site. They are fully editable and an excellent way to create usable items that you might want to change on a site-wide basis.

If you are used to using styles in a word processing or desktop publishing program then you will feel at home with HTML Styles.

HTML Styles

This brings up a window that displays the currently available pre-set styles that can be applied to text. Items of text can then be formatted by selecting one of the relevant styles. Existing styles can be edited and new ones can be created:

Cascading Style Sheets are an excellent way to change elements that occur on dozens of different pages. This can be done by changing the CSS and the new style will apply to all of the pages that have been set up in this way. This should be kept in mind when you are designing your pages — CSS Styles should be applied at the beginning of the design process if possible.

CSS Styles

This brings up a window that displays the currently available Cascading Style Sheets. This is a formatting technique that allows you to control the appearance of several different items on a page e.g. heading and body text, and even apply these styles to several pages simultaneously:

Behaviors

This brings up a window that displays small pieces of programming that perform certain tasks within the page. Behaviors consist of an action and an event that triggers it:

History

This brings up a window that displays a list of all of the editing functions that you have performed on the current document, such as typing and formatting text, inserting an image or resizing a table:

The History palette can be used to reapply actions that have been undertaken previously or to undo several actions that have already been performed. This can be useful if you have made a number of editing changes that you then want to remove. This can also be achieved with the Edit>Undo command from the menu bar, which allows you to undo multiple actions.

Code Source

This displays the source HTML code for the current page. It is possible to edit this code and any changes will also take effect in the Design view:

If the Code is accessed from the Launcher palette, this opens in a separate window and is known and the Code Inspector. It can also be accessed from Design view, either on its own or as a split screen with the contents of the Design view window

Any changes made in the source code window will also apply in the document window

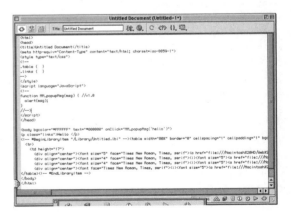

If you are comfortable using HTML, then the Code Source window can be used to hand-code your Web pages. Any changes that are made here will automatically appear when you return to the document window.

External editors

When designing Web pages, you will be working with a lot of elements that cannot be edited directly within Dreamweaver. The most obvious example of this is images, but it also applies to elements such as sound files or movie clips. One way to edit them would be to do so in an appropriate program before they are inserted into Dreamweaver. However, if you then need to edit the items again, once they have been imported, it can be frustrating having to open up the file again, edit it, and then re-import it. Dreamweaver simplifies this process by providing direct links to external programs that can be used to edit items while they are still in the Dreamweaver environment. This is know as using external editors.

The most commonly used external editors with Dreamweaver are for editing HTML code and editing images. HTML editing can be done with a text editor (such as NotePad on a PC or SimpleText on a Mac) and images can be edited with a graphics program such as Fireworks or Photoshop. Dreamweaver integrates very closely with Fireworks and so this is the best option when working with images, if possible.

It is possible to specify which program you want to use for specific tasks e.g. editing images, by selecting the file type and the program from the External Editors section of the Preferences window:

1 Select Edit> Preferences from the menu bar

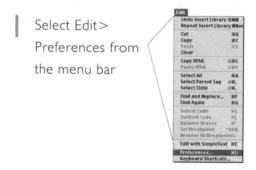

2 Click here to select a file type

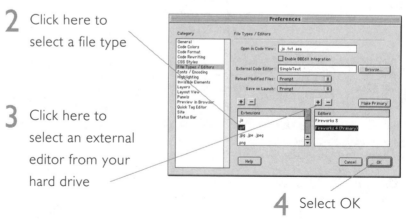

3 Click here to select an external editor from your hard drive

4 Select OK

Using external editors

Once you have selected the required external editors for different file formats, it is then possible to access them while you are working on a page:

I Select an element on a page, such as an image

Files have to be saved and named before their content can be edited using an external editor. If you try and do this without saving a file then a dialog box will appear asking you to do this.

2 Right-click (Windows) Ctrl+click (Mac) on the item and select Edit With to edit it with the primary external editor that has been assigned to this file type

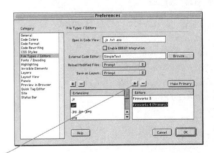

3 To change the external editor for a specific file type at any time, select Edit>Launch External Editor and change the selection in the External Editor dialog box, as shown on the facing page

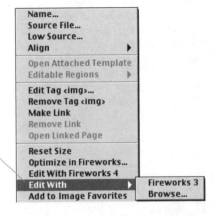

Page properties

In addition to setting preferences that affect all of the files you work on in Dreamweaver, it is also possible to set properties for individual pages. This includes items such as background colour, the colour of links and the margins on the page. To set page properties:

If you are using a background image on a Web page, make sure it is not too complex or gaudy. This could create a dramatic initial effect, but if people are looking at the page a lot it could become irritating. Similarly, background colours should, in general, be subtle and unobtrusive, rather than bright and bold. White is a very effective background for Web pages.

1 Select Modify> Page Properties from the menu bar

2 Click here to select a background image for the active page, from your hard drive

Hyperlinks, or just links, can be coloured differently depending on their current state. Different colours can be applied for a link before it has been activated, after it has been activated and when it is being pressed.

3 Click here to select a background colour for the active page

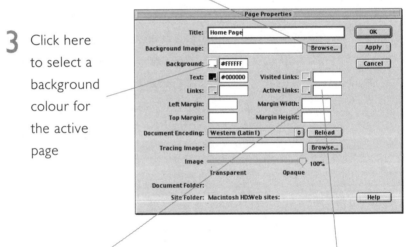

5 Click here to set the margins for the active page

4 Click here to select a colour for the links on the page

The Preview in Browser function can also be achieved by pressing the F12 key on the keyboard.

Menus and the toolbar

A lot of the menu functions can be accessed using keyboard shortcuts e.g. a file can be opened with Ctrl+O (Windows) Command+O (Mac). These shortcuts are displayed next to the relevant menu items.

Using menus

The menus that are contained within the menu bar at the top of Dreamweaver can be used to access all of the functions that are required to create multimedia-rich Web sites. Some of these functions, such as those on the Insert menu, are duplicated on the floating palettes and it is sometimes a question of personal preference as to how a certain action is accessed. There are dozens of elements contained within the Dreamweaver menus and they will be covered at the relevant points at which they occur throughout the book. To access the elements within a menu:

Contextual menus can be accessed for specific items. To do this, select the item and then right-click (Windows) or Ctrl+click (Mac) to view the relevant contextual menu i.e. the menu with options relating to the selected item.

Select a menu item. If there is an arrow next to it, click on it to see the relevant sub-menu options

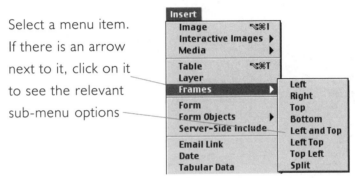

Toolbar

The toolbar at the top of the page has a number of options for specifying how Dreamweaver operates:

The Page view options on the toolbar allow you to switch between the graphical layout or the HTML layout, or a combination of the two. For more information on this, see Chapter Three.

Page views   Page Title   Refresh   Reference (see next page)

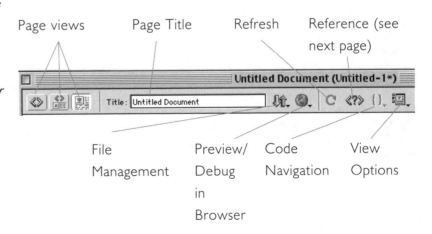

File Management   Preview/ Debug in Browser   Code Navigation   View Options

Getting help

The Help menu also has an option for registering your copy of Dreamweaver. This is done online by connecting to the Macromedia Web site and once you have gone through the registration process you will be able to get technical support for the product and also receive the latest information about updates and upgrades.

The Help files automatically open up in your default Web browser, usually either Internet Explorer or Netscape Navigator. It is recommended that version 4 or later of both browsers is used, or else some of the Help functions will not function fully. If you are using Dreamweaver on a Mac, Netscape Navigator 4 or later is recommended as Internet Explorer for the Mac will not be able to play the online demos.

If you need to upgrade your browser to a newer version this can be done by downloading them from the Microsoft or Netscape Web sites, at www.microsoft.com or www.netscape.com respectively.

In common with most software programs, Dreamweaver offers an extensive range of help items. These include a general help index, online demonstrations of using the program and Web sites for the latest upgrades.

Dreamweaver Help

The main help index is displayed in a browser window. This has a variety of options, all of which are accessed from the Help button on the menu bar:

O'Reilly Reference

A new innovation in Dreamweaver 4 is the use of the O'Reilly Reference feature. This is a help feature provided by the respected publishers O'Reilly. It provides detailed information about the selected item on the page. To access O'Reilly Reference, select an item on the page and click on this icon on the toolbar:

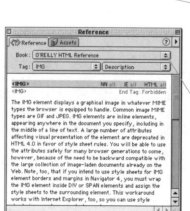

The Reference panel is displayed. Click here to access additional features

Setting up a site

Before you start creating Web pages it is important to set up a site structure into which all of your page content will be placed. This chapter looks at setting up a site, viewing the structure and the basics of creating, opening and saving files.

Covers

Planning a site | 30

Creating a new site | 31

Adding pages | 32

Saving files | 34

Opening files | 35

Switching between windows | 36

Setting a home page | 37

Viewing the site map | 39

Defining a site | 40

Chapter Two

Planning a site

Web sites that are published on the Internet are not just random pages that are thrown together in the hope that people will be able to view them over the Web. Instead, each site is a group of pages, images and, if applicable, multimedia effects, that are linked together by a structure that is invariably created before any of the pages are created. It is possible to create Web pages outside a Web structure in Dreamweaver and store them on your own computer. However, when it comes to creating a whole site it is important that you create a structure into which you can place all of the content for your site. When it comes to publishing your Web site on the Internet, you would encounter numerous problems if you had not already set up a site structure.

Do not try and create a new site in an existing folder that has other files in it. If you do, Dreamweaver will include all of these files in your site, even if they are not appropriate.

Preparing a structure

Before you start working with the site structure tools in Dreamweaver, it is a good idea to decide where you want to store your sites on your own hard drive. The pages and other content for a Web site are stored in a folder on your hard drive in exactly the same way as any other file. It is therefore a good idea to create a new folder for all of your Web authoring files. As you create sites, you can create sub-folders from the main folder for each new site. Also, for each site you may want to create sub-folders for all of the images in your site, and the suchlike. If you do this before you start creating your Web pages, it will make it easier to save and add pages to a site. Once you have set up your folder structure it could look something like this:

Draw a rough sketch of your proposed site structure before you start creating folders and files. This does not have to be the definitive structure, but it will give you a good overview of what you are trying to achieve.

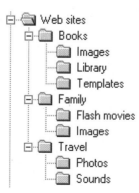

Creating a new site

After you have created a folder structure for your Web sites, you can begin to create individual sites within Dreamweaver. Once a site has been created, the content can then be added and built upon. If all of the items are stored within the same site structure you will be able to perform a variety of site management tasks with Dreamweaver. To set up a new site:

You can create as many different structures for different Web sites as you like. But make sure each one has its own root folder.

1 In the main document window, select Site> New Site from the menu bar

Try and give your sites easily identifiable names, rather than just My Site or Web Site. If you are going to be creating a lot of Web sites, this is particularly important so that you can quickly identify which is which.

2 In the Site Definition dialog box, enter the name for the new site here

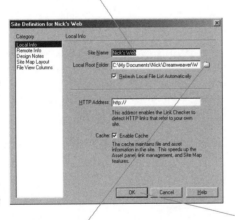

After you select OK, in Step 4, a dialog box appears asking if you want to create a cache. This is a method of storing information so that it can be accessed more quickly. It is advisable to select Create.

3 Click here to browse your hard drive for the folder in which the new site will be stored. This should be one of the folders that have already been set up as shown on the previous page. This is known as the root folder for the site

4 Select OK

Adding pages

Once you have created a new site, and selected OK, as described on the previous page, the site window will appear. This displays the files that are contained within the current site:

The site window displays the items contained within the current site. When a site is first created there is only the root folder. The folders on the hard drive are known as Local folders — once they are transferred onto the Web they are known as Remote folders

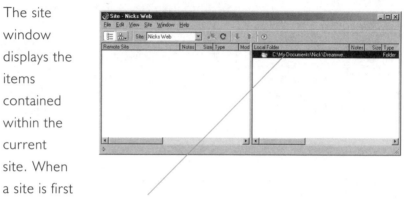

While you are working on files within your Web site during the authoring process, they should always be only stored in your local folder i.e. on your own computer. They should only be copied to remote folders i.e. the server hosting your site, when you are ready to publish your site. When this is done, the remote folders should be a mirror image of the local ones.

The next step is to start adding pages to your new Web site. There are two ways of doing this:

Adding pages through the site window

New pages can be added directly from the site window once a site has been created. To do this:

A server is basically a large computer that is configured to store Web sites and deal with requests to view them by users.

Select the folder within the site where you want to create the new page

When you enter the name for a new file in the site window, make sure you include the file extension i.e. '–.htm' or '–.html'. Otherwise Dreamweaver will not be able to recognise the file type and will therefore not be able to open it.

2 Select File>New File (Windows) File>New (Mac) from the menu bar

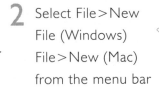

3 Type a name for the new file and open it by double-clicking on the Dreamweaver icon

Adding pages from Design view

A new page can also be created by pressing Ctrl+N (Windows) or Command+N (Mac) on the keyboard.

1 In Design view, select File>New from the menu bar

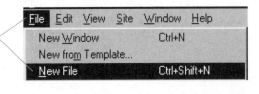

A document's file name appears at the top left of the screen next to the Dreamweaver icon. Initially this will say 'Untitled Document (Untitled-1)'. The Untitled Document refers to the page title, which can be added by selecting Modify>Page Properties from the menu bar and entering a name for the page in the Title box. This is included in the pages Head information.

The Untitled-1 refers to the file's name and this changes once it has been saved and given a unique file name.

2 A new blank file opens in Design view. At this point it has no content and is untitled. Once the content has been added the file has to be saved into the required file within the site structure (see overleaf)

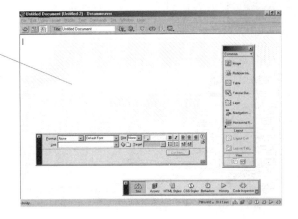

Saving files

If a new file has been created through Design view it has to be saved within the required folder in the site structure so that Dreamweaver can identify it as part of a particular site. If a new file has been created in the site window then it only needs to be saved, because it will already be within a site structure. To save a new file created in Design view:

Files and pages are interchangeable terms when it comes to Web authoring

1 Select File > Save (or Save As) from the menu bar

Either Save or Save As can be used if it is the first time a file has been saved — the same dialog box appears.

2 In the Save As dialog box, locate the required site and folder where you want the new file saved. Enter a name for the new file

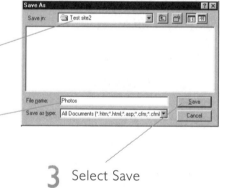

3 Select Save

A file has to be saved before it can be used within a site structure and use the functions that are available here.

Once a file has been saved within a site structure it can then be edited and have more content added to it. Any changes can be saved by selecting File > Save from the menu bar. Since the file has already been saved to a folder within a site structure, there is no need to specify the exact location of where the file is to be saved each time.

Make sure you save your work regularly, because if the program crashes you will lose everything that you have done since the last Save.

Opening files

Existing files can be opened from either the site window or Design view.

Opening files from the site window

A selected file in the site window can also be opened by right-clicking (Windows) or Ctrl+clicking (Mac) on it and selecting Open from the contextual menu.

1 Click here to select a site

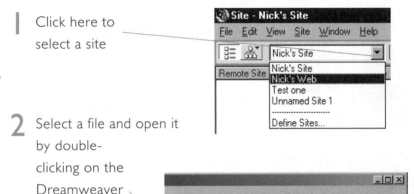

2 Select a file and open it by double-clicking on the Dreamweaver icon or by selecting File>Open from the menu bar

It is possible to open several files at once by selecting them all in the site window (by holding down Ctrl and clicking on the files you want to select) and then right-clicking (Windows) or Ctrl+clicking (Mac) and selecting Open from the contextual menu.

Opening files from Design view

1 Select File>Open from the menu bar

If the root folder is selected in the site window, the Open dialog box appears when Open is selected. Select a file as you would when opening a file from Design view.

2 In the Open dialog box, locate the required site and file. Select Open

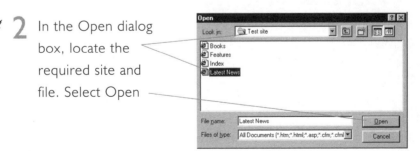

Switching between windows

When you are working on the files within a Web site, there will be times when you will want to work in Design view, and others when you will want to work with your site structure in the site window. It is therefore important to be able to switch quickly between the two. To do this:

Switching to the site window

The site window is where you can perform various site management tasks. For more on this, see Chapter Twelve.

In Design view, select Site>Site Files from the menu bar (Windows) or Site>Open Site and select a Site (Mac)

or

Select Window>Site Files from the menu bar (Windows and Mac)

Switching to Design view

You can toggle between Design view and the site window by pressing F8 (Windows and Mac).

In the site window, select File>New Window (Windows) or File>New (Mac)

or

Select Window and select the file you want to open from the open files list

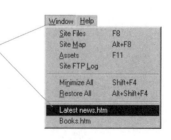

Setting a home page

Every Web site has to have a home page. This is the one that appears when the site is first accessed and as far as the browser viewing the site is concerned, everything within the site is created relative to the home page. This can be particularly important when you are performing certain site management tasks, because Dreamweaver needs to know what is the home page, to use this as a reference point. There are two ways to define a home page in Dreamweaver:

From the Site Definition window

The home page can be specified in the Site Definition window when a site is first defined or it can be edited once the site has been created. Either way, the process for specifying the home page is the same:

Name the home page in each Dreamweaver site, 'index.htm' or 'index.html'. They can be given other names, but these are the ones that work most effectively within Dreamweaver.

The Site Definition window can be accessed from either Design view or the site window. For both, select Site>Define Sites from the menu bar. Then, in the Define Sites dialog box, select the required site and select Edit to access the Site Definition window.

1 In the Site Definition window, select Site Map Layout

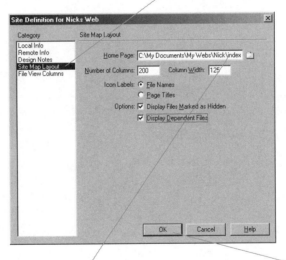

2 Click here to enter a file name for the home page or click on the folder icon to browse for a home page in the Choose Home Page dialog box

3 Select OK

From the site window

1 Make sure you are in the Site Files view by clicking here

Get into the habit of naming a home page at the same time as any new sites are created.

2 Select the file that you want to use as the home page

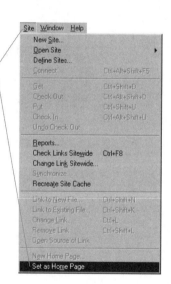

You can also set the home page by right-clicking (Windows) or Ctrl+clicking (Mac) on a file and selecting Set as Home Page from the contextual menu.

3 Select Site > Set as Home Page (Windows) or Site > Site Map View > Set as Home Page (Mac) from the menu bar

Viewing the site map

The site map is a Web site management tool that displays a graphical representation of all of the files in the current site and the way that they relate to each other. Each file in the site map is defined in relation to the home page. This is one reason why it is important to specify a home page. The site map shows the links between various files within the current site and also any files that have broken links. To access the site map:

Hyperlinks are the device used on Web pages to link to one another, through the use of a piece of HTML code. Links can be broken if a file name is changed or a file is moved to another location without updating the link. The site map displays any broken links within a site, allowing the designer to take remedial action with the relevant files. For more information on hyperlinks, see Chapter Seven.

The site map can be used to view how all of the pages on a site interact with each other. For more information on this, see Chapter Twelve.

1 Click here in the site window to view the site map

2 If you have not already specified a home page, the following dialog box

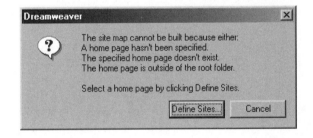

will appear. Select Define Sites to select a home page as shown on page 37

3 The site map displays the file hierarchy

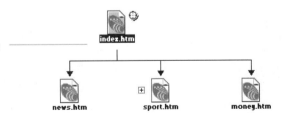

Defining a site

A site can be defined when it is first created and it is also possible to change these settings once a site has been set up. To create or edit the definition of a site:

1 Select Site > Define Sites from the menu bar (or Site > New Site if you want to create and define a new site)

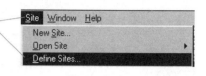

The other category in the Site Definition box is Remote Info. This covers aspects of publishing a site and is looked at in more detail in Chapter Twelve.

2 Select the site you want to define and select Edit in the Define Sites dialog box

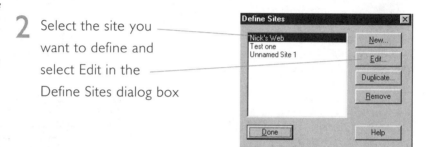

3 Enter details here to change the name or root location of the site

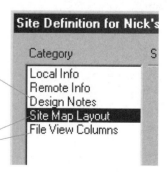

Design Notes is a function that allows designers to add notes to Web pages as they are working on them. This can be particularly useful if a team of designers are working on the same site.

4 Click here to select the options for using Design Notes within a site

5 Click here to select options affecting the layout of the Site Map

HTML in Dreamweaver

This chapter looks at the options that Dreamweaver provides for adding and editing HTML (HyperText Markup Language) code, which is used to create Web pages. It shows how to create your own code, either within Dreamweaver or in an external editor, and also explains how to work with HTML without leaving the main authoring environment.

Covers

HTML overview | 42

Page views | 44

HTML preferences | 45

Roundtrip HTML | 48

Rewriting preferences | 50

Invalid code | 51

Cleaning up HTML | 52

Cleaning up Word HTML | 53

Quick Tag editor | 54

Quick Tag preferences | 57

Selecting and removing tags | 58

Chapter Three

HTML overview

HyperText Markup Language (HTML) is the computer code used to create Web pages. It is not a fully-blown computer programming language, but rather a set of instructions that enables a Web browser to determine the layout of pages.

HTML is created by using a series of tags, which contain the instructions that are interpreted by the browsers. These tags are placed around the item to which you want that particular command to apply. Most tags, but not all of them, have an opening and a closing element. The opening tag contains the particular command and the closing tag contains the same command, but with a / in front of it, to denote the end of the command. For instance, if you wanted to display a piece of text as bold, you could do it with the following piece of HTML:

For more detailed information about HTML, take a look at 'HTML in easy steps'.

This text would appear bold in a browser

HTML is a text based code which means that the source HTML file only contains text and not any images or multimedia items. These appear in the browser because of a reference to them that is placed in an HTML document. For instance, if you wanted to include an image in a document you would insert the following piece of HTML into your source file:

<img src="myimage.jpg">

For more complex functions on a Web page, there is a language called Dynamic Hypertext Markup Language (DHTML). This requires some programming knowledge in order to write it, although some DHTML functions can be inserted directly onto a page.

This would instruct the browser to insert this image at the required point within the HTML document when it is being viewed on the Web. It is possible to insert HTML code to instruct a variety of graphics and multimedia files to be displayed in a Web page. However, it is important to remember that when you are publishing your pages, all of the items that are referred to in the source HTML document are uploaded to the server as well as the HTML file.

Since Dreamweaver is a What You See Is What You Get (WYSIWYG) program, it generates all of the HTML in the background. This means that it is possible to ignore its existence completely. However, it is useful to learn the basics.

Underlined text should only be used as a design feature on Web pages in exceptional circumstances. This is because hyperlinks (the device used to move to other pages and Web sites) usually appear underlined to denote their status. If normal text is also underlined, this could cause confusion.

For more information about images on Web pages, see Chapter Six.

Tables are an excellent way to format a variety of different content on a Web page. They do not just have to be used for formatting words or figures. For more information about tables, see Chapter Eight.

Common tags

Some of the most commonly used tags in HTML are (unless otherwise stated, they all use the equivalent closing tag by inserting / in front of the command):

- \<p> This creates a new paragraph

- \<b> This creates bold text

- \<i> This creates italics

- \<u> This creates underlined text

- \
 This inserts a line break (this does not have a closing tag)

- \<hr> This inserts a horizontal line (this does not have a closing tag)

- \<img src="image.jpg"> This inserts the specified image

- \<font face="Arial"> This specifies a certain font. The closing tag is just \</font>

- \<h1> This formats text at a preset heading size. There are six levels for this: h1 being the largest and h6 being the smallest. Paragraph and other formatting tags cannot be used within heading tags

- \<table> This inserts a table

- \<color="ffffff"> This can be used to select a colour for a variety of items, including background colour and text colour

- \<a href="default.htm">Home Page\</a> This is used to create a hyperlink to another Web page. In this case the link is to the file 'default.htm' and the words 'Home Page' will appear underlined on the Web page, denoting that it is a link to another page

Page views

Code view can be accessed from the Design view toolbar, and the Code Inspector can be accessed from the Launcher. They both bring up the same information, but Code view opens in the same window, while Code Inspector opens in a separate one.

Although it is possible to be blissfully unaware of the existence of HTML when you are using Dreamweaver, you can also hand-code pages using Code view or the Code Inspector. This allows you to create your own HTML code, which is then translated into the document window by Dreamweaver. This can be a good way to learn about HTML and perform fine tuning tasks if you cannot achieve it through the document window. In Dreamweaver 4 you can access the graphical version of the page; the HTML code on its own; or a combination of them both:

Click here to access the Code view and the Design view together.

Click here to access the Design view on its own

When Code view and Design view are showing together, if any changes are made to one of these views, the other is updated automatically

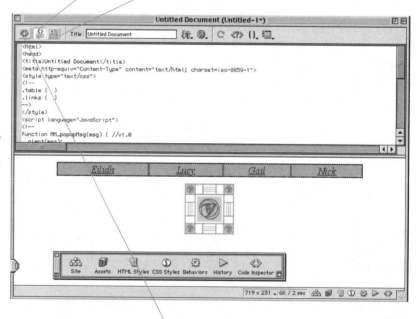

Click here to access the Code view on its own

HTML preferences

Code colours

When creating and editing HTML within Dreamweaver, it is possible to set various defaults for the colours within the HTML Source window. This can not only be useful for aesthetic reasons, but also to make specific elements stand out within the code. These elements can then be quickly identified when working with the source code. To set the preferences for colours within the Code Source window:

Use a consistent theme for colours within the HTML

Source window, so that you can easily recognise different elements within the code even if you are working on different Web sites.

1 Select Edit>Preferences from the menu bar

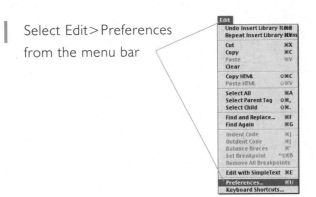

2 Select Code Colors in the Preferences dialog box

As with all of the colour palettes within Dreamweaver, it is possible to

apply a wider range of colours for the HTML options than the ones on the standard palette that appears. Click on the paint palette at the bottom right-corner to create your own custom colours.

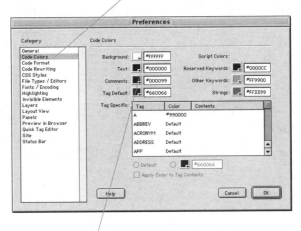

3 Click here to access the colour palette for the various options

The options for setting colours within the HTML Source window are:

- Background. This affects the background colour of the window

- Text. This affects the colour of the text that appears in the document

- Comments. This affects the colour of any comments that you insert into the HTML code. These are not displayed in the published document

- Tag Default. This affects the default colour for HTML tags

- Tag Specific. This allows you to set specific colours to be assigned to individual HTML tags. This can be a useful way to identify certain elements within the HTML code, such as hyperlinks. To set the Tag Specific preferences:

The Comments option is a device that allows Web designers to add comments to a page while they are working on it. This could be something like 'Add an image of the boss here' or a comment for any other designers who may be working on the page at some stage.

A comment is denoted in the document window with an invisible tag (select View>Invisible Elements to see them in the document window) and in the HTML source it appears within angled brackets and with an exclamation mark and two dashes before and after it. The colour for this can be set in the HTML Colors window, so that any comments are clearly identified in the source code.

Comments can be added in the document window by selecting Insert>Comment from the menu bar and they do not appear in the published page.

Select a tag from this list

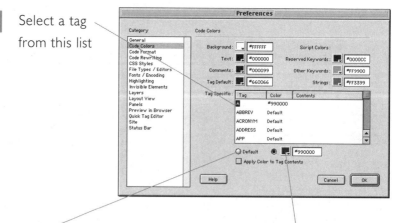

2 Click here to use the default colour

3 Click here to select a colour from the colour swatch

Code format

These preferences can be used to determine the layout of the code within the HTML Source window. These include the format for how tags are presented and also the use of indents and tabs to indicate certain elements, such as tables and frames. To access the Code Format preferences:

According to the values that are set, different elements on a page will be displayed with code that is indented in the HTML Source. For instance, the code for table rows and columns and frames is usually indented.

Select Code Format from the Preferences dialog box

Click here to specify how indents are displayed and which items will appear indented

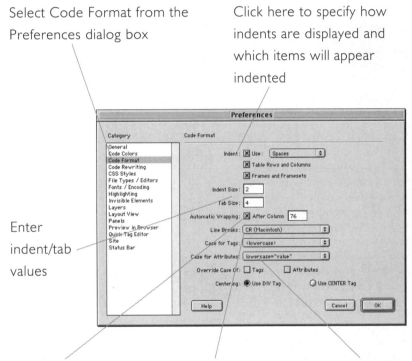

Enter indent/tab values

Before you start creating Web pages, decide whether you want your tags to be in upper or lower case. Once you have done this, stick to it for all of your pages and sites, for the sake of consistency. In general, lowercase tags are neater and take up less room.

Specify text wrapping i.e. how many characters before the text is moved to the next line

Click here to determine how different servers on the Web deal with line breaks within your source code

Specify if tags and attributes are displayed in upper or lower case

Roundtrip HTML

Roundtrip HTML is a feature unique to Dreamweaver that allows you to edit your source code in an external text editor and then automatically update the changes in the Dreamweaver document. It is even possible to set a variety of preferences so that Dreamweaver will correct any coding or syntax errors that have occurred while you have been editing the document in an external editor. This can be useful if you are used to working with a text editor, such as NotePad on a PC or SimpleText on a Mac. In addition to using these types of editor for HTML coding it is also possible to use them for more complicated programming such as JavaScript and VB Script, if you are so inclined.

A file has to be saved and placed within a site structure before an external editor can be used to edit the HTML code.

You can use Roundtrip HTML in either Dreamweaver itself (using Code view or the Code Inspector) or you can access an external HTML editor, write the relevant code, and then import it back into Dreamweaver.

Code view can be accessed as shown on page 44. In addition, the Code Inspector can also be launched. This works in the same way as Code view, except it launches in its own window. To access the Code Inspector:

In addition to plain text editors, more advanced HTML editors can also be used as external editors. These are programs that still work with the source HTML code, but they provide a variety of functions for creating it more quickly. A lot of these programs are free and can be downloaded from the Web.

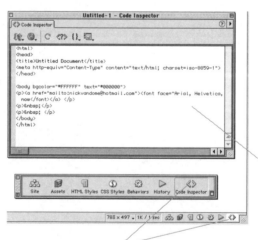

Click here to access the Code Inspector, which opens in its own window. The HTML code can then be edited, and these changes will appear in the Design view

Using an external HTML editor

The Windows version of Dreamweaver 4 comes with Homesite as an external HTML editor. This can be used if you do not want to use Notepad.

On the Mac only, a popular external editor, BBEdit (BB stands for Bare Bones), is included with Dreamweaver. If you want to use another external editor on the Mac, deselect the Enable BBEdit Integration option in the External Editors window.

Editing changes can also be made in Code view or Code Inspector within Dreamweaver itself. However, some external editors may have a wider range of features.

1 Select Edit>Edit with... from the menu bar. If no external text editor has been selected the choices will be SimpleText (Mac) or Notepad (Windows). To select a different editor see page 24

2 The file will open up in the external editor specified in Step 1

3 Make changes to your HTML or add new code.

Once you have saved any changes and returned to Dreamweaver, the following window will appear. Select Yes to make the changes active in your Dreamweaver document

Rewriting preferences

If you are using an external editor to create or edit HTML, or if you want to open an HTML document that was created in another application, there are preferences that can be set in Dreamweaver that instruct the program to amend any items of incorrect coding that are in the document. However, these changes are not made to any code created in the HTML Source window within Dreamweaver. To set rewriting preferences:

Options can also be set for not rewriting HTML for files with specific extensions and for encoding special characters. Unless you have good reason not to, it is best to leave these boxes checked on.

1 Select Edit>Preferences from the menu bar

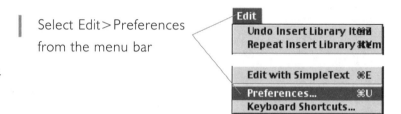

2 Select Code Rewriting in the Preferences dialog box

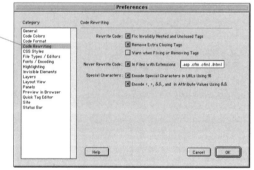

Some browsers will still be able to display HTML pages even if they contain invalidly nested or unclosed tags. However, it is technically incorrect and can cause problems in certain situations.

The rewriting options are:

- Fix Invalidly Nested or Unclosed tags. This rearranges nested tags (i.e. two or more together, that are in the wrong order) and inserts closing tags if they are missing

- Remove Extra Closing Tags. This deletes any superfluous closing tags

- Warn when Fixing or Removing Tags. This activates a warning box when the rewriting options are performed

Invalid code

If you write any invalid code in the HTML Source window, or turn off all of the HTML Rewriting preferences when opening a document from another source, any invalid code will be highlighted in yellow, in both the HTML Source window and the document window. This means that Dreamweaver has encountered some code that it does not understand and therefore it cannot display it correctly or reformat it automatically. However, it is possible to manually correct any invalid code:

On occasions, a whole string of HTML tags will be marked as being invalid. However, this can sometimes be corrected by fixing one tag, such as changing its nesting order.

If you are familiar with HTML, it can be quicker to fix invalid code in the Code view window rather than Design view.

If you encounter any invalid code on your pages, press F12 to see how this affects the page when it is viewed in a browser. In some cases it will be noticeable.

1 Click on the yellow tags that denote invalid HTML code. This can be done in either the Code view window or Design view

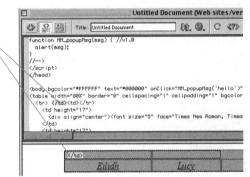

2 A window will appear alerting you to the reasons for the invalid code and instructing you how to repair it. Follow these instructions and check that the yellow tags have subsequently disappeared:

Cleaning up HTML

If you can make your HTML code as clean as possible, you may gain greater respect from any HTML experts who look at your source code when your pages are on the Web.

One of the problems with WYSIWYG Web authoring programs is that they tend to create a certain amount of superfluous or redundant HTML coding. Although Dreamweaver is more efficient in this respect than a lot of similar programs it does still produce some unnecessary code. This results in files not being as 'clean' as possible. This does not necessarily have an effect on the way a Web page looks, but it can create larger file sizes. Generally the more complex that a design is, then the more unnecessary HTML code will be created.

Dreamweaver has a facility for checking the source HTML code in documents, to ensure that it is as clean as possible. To do this:

The options that can be selected within the Clean Up HTML dialog box are:

* *Remove empty tags*
* *Remove Redundant Nested Tags*
* *Remove Non-Dreamweaver HTML Comments*
* *Remove Dreamweaver HTML Comments*
* *Remove Specific Tags*
* *Combine Nested Tags when Possible*
* *Show Log on Completion*

1 Open a page in the document window and select Commands > Clean Up HTML from the menu bar

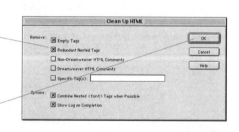

2 Check on the boxes for the clean up functions that you want to apply. Click OK to apply them

3 A dialog box will appear informing you of the clean up operations that have been performed. Select OK

Cleaning up Word HTML

In addition to dedicated Web authoring programs, some more advanced word processing programs have a function for converting documents into an HTML format. The most commonly used in this respect is Microsoft Word. While this can be an effective way to convert textual documents into HTML, it can be a bit hit and miss when more complex designs are being used. It also tends to create a lot of redundant HTML, even more so than when using a specific HTML program. Dreamweaver recognises the fact that a lot of users will be creating HTML pages with Word and it has a function for cleaning up code that was produced by this specific program:

Word is notorious for inserting a lot of unnecessary code when it creates HTML pages. Therefore, if you are using Word HTML pages, make sure you use the Clean Up option when you are working with the page in Dreamweaver.

The options that can be selected within the Clean Up Word HTML dialog box are:

- Remove all Word specific markup
- Clean up CSS
- Clean up <font> tags
- Fix invalidly nested tags
- Set background colour
- Apply source formatting
- Show log on completion

The options above are the basic Clean Up Word HTML commands. An Advanced tab can also be selected for a wider range of options.

1 Open a page in the document window and select Commands>Clean Up Word HTML from the menu bar

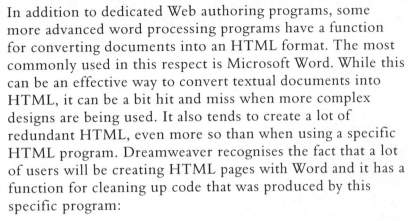

2 Select the version of Word in which the file was created and select the clean up functions that you want to apply

3 A dialog box will appear informing you of the clean up operations that have been performed. Select OK

Quick Tag editor

When editing HTML code there will probably be times when you want to quickly change or add a specific tag. This can be done by accessing the HTML Source window. However, it is also possible to do this without leaving the document window, through the use of the Quick Tag editor. This is a function that enables you to insert and check HTML tags directly in the document window. Any changes that are made are updated automatically in the HTML Source window. The Quick Tag editor can be accessed by selecting Modify>Quick Tag Editor from the menu bar or by using Ctrl+T (Windows) or Command+T (Mac). This shortcut can also be used to toggle between the different modes of the Quick Tag editor.

There are three different modes that can be used within the Quick Tag editor:

Insert HTML mode

This enables you to insert new HTML tags into a document. If required it can be used to insert a string of several tags together. If the closing tags are not inserted, then Dreamweaver will place these automatically in the most appropriate place.

When inserting tags with the Quick Tag editor it is best to also insert the corresponding closing tag at the required point. Check in the HTML Source window to make sure that the tags have been inserted in the correct places.

Insert HTML mode can be used to insert both opening and closing tags and also the content in between them.

Once tags have been entered in the Quick Tag the changes can be applied by clicking back in the document window.

1 Insert the cursor at the point where you want to create a new HTML tag. Do not select any elements on the page

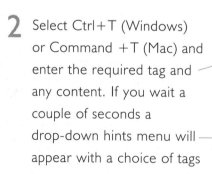

My passport photo

2 Select Ctrl+T (Windows) or Command +T (Mac) and enter the required tag and any content. If you wait a couple of seconds a drop-down hints menu will appear with a choice of tags to use

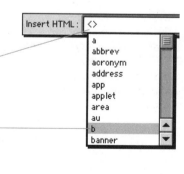

Edit Tag mode

This can be used to edit existing HTML tags in a document. The Quick Tag editor opens in this mode if an item with an opening and closing tag is selected on the page:

The Quick Tag editor can also be accessed by clicking on this icon on the Properties Inspector:

I Select an element on the page that contains an opening tag, content and a closing tag. This could include selecting an image, or an entire piece of formatted text

2 Select Ctrl+T (Windows) or Command +T (Mac) to open the Quick Tag editor in Edit Tag mode

Edit Tag: `<img src="file:///Macintosh%20HD/Desktop%20Folder/Passport%20photos/Lucy" width="177" height="140">`

In Edit Tag mode, you can edit tags manually i.e. write the HTML tags yourself, or insert a new tag from the hints menu that appears after a couple of seconds.

3 Edit the tag and then apply the changes by clicking within the document window

Edit Tag: `<img src="file:///Macintosh%20HD/Desktop%20Folder/Passport%20photos/Lucy" width="60" height="45">`

4 If you enter an incorrect tag, you will be alerted to this:

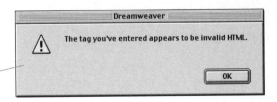

Dreamweaver

The tag you've entered appears to be invalid HTML.

OK

Wrap mode

This is the mode that the Quick Tag editor opens in if an incomplete tag and content is selected i.e. only part of a formatted piece of text. The Wrap mode allows you to insert a single tag but not a string of several tags. The tag is inserted at the beginning of the selection and a closing tag is inserted at the end of it. This can be a useful option for inserting a single tag within an existing HTML tag. To access the Wrap mode:

The Quick Tag editor can always be accessed by pressing Ctrl+T (Windows) or Command+T (Mac). The mode in which it opens up in is dependent on the selection that is made in the document window.

1   Select an element on the page that does not contain an entire tag

My passport **photo**

2   Select Ctrl+T (Windows) or Command +T (Mac) to open the Quick Tag editor in Wrap mode

Wrap Tag: <>

If you try and enter more than one tag in Wrap mode, an error message will appear and everything except the first tag will be ignored.

3   Edit the tag and then apply the changes by clicking within the document window

My passport **photo**

Wrap Tag: <i>

My passport **photo**

Quick Tag preferences

The Quick Tag editor has preferences that can be set to determine how it handles changes that are made to HTML when working in the document window. To set the Quick Tag preferences:

Select Edit>Preferences from the menu bar

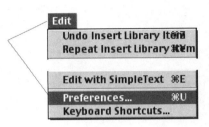

The Apply Changes Immediately While Editing preference does not apply to Insert or Wrap mode. For both of these Enter has to be pressed to apply any changes, or you can click back in the document window.

2 In the Preferences dialog box, select Quick Tag Editor

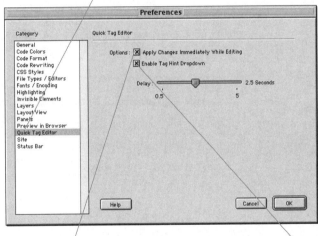

If you drag the Enable Tag Hints Delay button to the left hand side of the scale, the hints menu will appear almost immediately after accessing the Quick Tag editor in Insert or Wrap mode.

Check this box on if you want the changes made when in Edit mode to be applied immediately. If this is checked off the changes will only apply when you press Enter or click in the document window

Check this box on to enable the drop-down list of HTML tags when in the Quick Tag modes. Adjust the slider to specify the time delay before the list appears

Selecting and removing tags

Selecting tags

In addition to selecting tags by highlighting them in the document window it is also possible to select them from the tag selector which is located at the bottom left of the document window. This enables you to easily identify the opening and closing tags and also the content which is contained within them. To select tags using the tag selector:

Some tags appear in the tag selector when items are selected by clicking on them in the document window. Others, such as the body tag, are visible all of the time.

1 The relevant tags are displayed in the tag selector, which is located at the bottom left of the document window

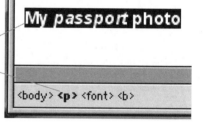

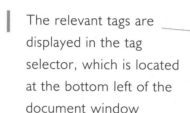

The tags displayed in the tag selector can also be used to access the Quick Tag Edit mode. To do this, right-click (Windows) or Ctrl+click (Mac) on the required tag in the tag selector — the Quick Tag editor will open in Edit mode, using the highlighted tag.

2 Select a tag by clicking on it once. The equivalent item is highlighted in the document window. This can then be edited using the Quick Tag editor

Removing tags

Right-click (Windows) or Ctrl+click (Mac) on one of the tags in the tag selector and select Remove Tag from the contextual menu

Assets

The process of creating Web sites can involve using the same basic designs and elements several times over. This chapter explains how Dreamweaver allows the Web designer to use commonly used items across a Web site, through the use of the Assets panel. Two of the most powerful of these items are templates and the Library, which are looked at in detail.

Covers

Managing assets | 60

Using templates | 62

Creating templates | 63

Editing templates | 65

Creating editable regions | 66

Template properties | 67

Creating pages from templates | 69

Updating pages based on templates | 70

About the Library | 71

Creating Library items | 72

Adding items from the Library | 73

Editing Library items | 74

Creating editable navigation bars | 76

Chapter Four

Managing assets

The Assets panel is an area that keeps track of many of the elements that you use in creating your Web sites. This includes:

The Assets panel will only show items for sites that have been defined. Once this has been done the Assets panel can recognise the items in the site's cache.

- Images

- Colours

- Hyperlinks

- Flash and Shockwave content

- Video

- Scripts

- Templates

- Library items

Using the colour assets is a good way to help achieve a consistent design throughout a Web site. Colours can easily be used on multiple pages, without having to remember the exact one each time.

You do not have to add items to the Assets panel (except for templates and Library items) since all of the relevant content is automatically inserted into the Assets panel when it is inserted into the Dreamweaver page. There are two ways to manage Assets: either on a site-wide basis, or as Favorites, which are usually items that you want to use on several pages. To view the site assets:

Click here on the Launcher or mini-Launcher

The Assets panel can also be accessed by selecting Window>Assets from the menu bar.

Check on the Site button and click on the Refresh button to view the assets for the current site

Creating Favorites

Assets that are going to be used regularly, such as an image that will appear on all the pages of a site, or a hyperlink back to the home page, can be added to the Favorites list for quick access. To do this:

The Favorites list can also be used to add new assets such as colours or hyperlinks.

Select an asset in the Site list and click here to add it to the Favorites
OR
Select an item in Design view and right-click (Windows) or Ctrl+click (Mac) and select the relevant Add To command

To remove an asset from the Favorites list, select it in the Favorites panel and then click here:

Applying assets

Assets are applied slightly differently depending on the item:

Assets can also be applied by dragging them from the Assets panel onto a page in Design view.

For images, Flash, Shockwave, video and scripts, select the item and then select Insert to place it on the page

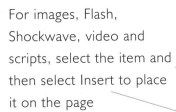

Templates and Library items behave slightly differently from other assets. These are dealt with in the rest of this chapter.

For colours and links, select the relevant item in Design view, then select the asset and select Apply to have it take effect on the page

Using templates

Template files have been a common feature in word processing and desktop publishing program for several years now. These are files that contain standard elements that recur in certain types of documents. The template can then be used to store the recurring items, and new content can also be added once a document is opened using the template as a foundation. This is an excellent device for producing a consistent design for items such as newsletters and brochures and it is also a timesaving device because the basic design only has to be created once.

Recognising the value of templates for Web designers, Dreamweaver now has the facility for creating and using templates. This means that designers can quickly create a consistent theme for a Web site, while still retaining the freedom to add new content to pages.

Templates in Dreamweaver can be created from scratch or existing files can be converted into templates. New files can then be created, based on an existing template. It is also possible to edit the content of template files.

When templates are created you can specify which areas are constant e.g. a company logo, and which are editable. This gives you a good degree of control over the pages that are created from your templates.

When a new document is opened from a template the document is based on the template, rather than being the template file itself. When it is first opened, the document will display the same content as the template file, but new items can then be added.

If a document has been created based on an existing template, this is shown by a tag here:

The colours for the tags in templates can be changed by selecting Edit>Preferences from the menu bar and then selecting Highlighting and a colour for each of the regions within the template. See page 68 for more details.

Some areas in a document created from a template remain static and cannot be edited, while others are fully editable. Editable regions are denoted by a blue tag, with the name of the region

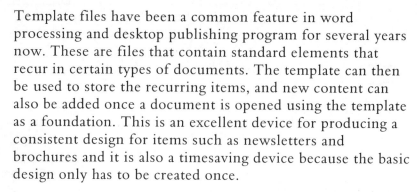

Creating templates

Templates can be created from scratch or existing files can be converted into templates.

Creating a new template

A template is identified in the document window with the word <<*Template*>> *before its name.*

1 Select Window> Templates from the menu bar

2 In the Assets panel click here and click here to create a new template

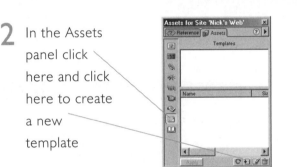

3 Give the new template a name and then click here to open the template

Dreamweaver templates are created with a '–.dwt' extension rather than a '–.htm' one.

4 Add the template's content and select File>Save or Save as Template

Creating a template from an existing document

1 Open the document you want to use as a template

2 Select File>Save
as Template

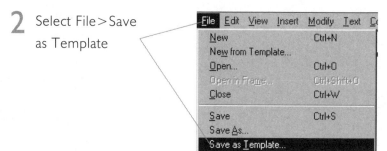

It is only possible to start creating editable regions once a document has been saved as a template.

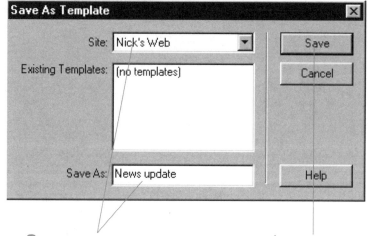

When a file is saved as a template the original is also retained. This means that you can save as many files as you like from a template, safe in the knowledge that the original version will still be intact.

When templates are created, they are placed within the current site structure, as separate files and usually in a specific template folder.

3 In the Save As Template dialog box, select a site for the template and give it a name

4 Select Save

Editing templates

If you want to change the content of a particular template, this can be done by editing it. This changes the content for all of the documents that have been based on this template. So if you have ten documents based on a single template, the size of the headings in each one could be altered by editing the heading formatting in the template file. To edit a template:

1 Select Window> Templates from the menu bar

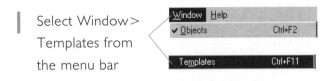

2 Select a template and open it by double-clicking on it, or clicking here

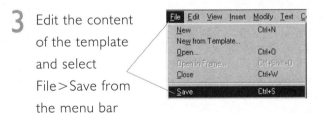

If you are updating a template, check all of the files to which it is linked, to make sure that you want to make the intended editing change to all of them. If you do not, you can detach any of the files from the template by opening them and selecting Modify>Templates>Detach from Template from the menu bar.

3 Edit the content of the template and select File>Save from the menu bar

4 A dialog box will appear asking if you want to update all of the documents based on this template. If you do, select Update

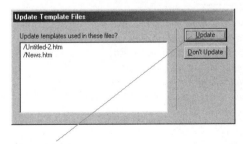

Creating editable regions

When a template is created, or an existing document is saved as a template, all of the content in the document is, by default, locked. This means that when a new document based on the template is opened, it will not be possible to change any elements on the page, or add more content. This is obviously of limited use if you want to create pages with different content based on the same template. Dreamweaver therefore makes it possible to mark certain regions within a template as editable. This means that when a new document is based on this template, the editable regions can be amended and have new content added to them. It is possible to select an existing element within a template and make it editable, or create a new, blank editable region.

If you want to convert an existing document into a template, this has to be done first, before any editable regions can be added.

Making an element editable

To make an existing piece of text or a graphic editable:

Create editable regions for items such as headings, body text, lists and indexes.

| Open a template and select the item that you want to make editable

Global Web

Here is the latest breaking news:

Heading 1

Sub heading

New editable regions can be created in a similar way to making an existing item in a template editable. Instead of selecting an item, insert the cursor at the point where you want the new editable region and then follow steps 2 and 3.

2 Select Modify > Templates > New Editable Region from the menu bar

3 In the New Editable Region dialog box, give the editable region a name. Click OK

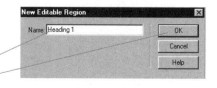

Template properties

Templates can have properties assigned to them in exactly the same way as standard pages. These properties are set in the Page Properties dialog box for the template. Once these properties are set they will apply to any documents that are created from the template and they will not be able to be altered in the documents's page properties. The exception to this is the page title. To set a template's properties:

1 Open a template then select Modify> Page Properties from the menu bar

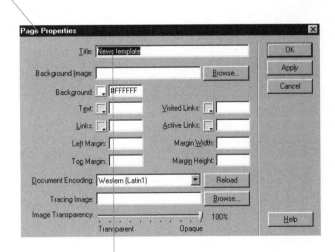

2 Enter the properties that you want to apply to this template. These will also apply to any documents that are based on this template

By setting the page properties for a template it is possible to change an element for several pages at once just by altering it in the template. For instance, if 20 pages are based on a template that has a background colour set to blue, all of these pages can have their backgrounds changed to red simply by updating the background colour in the template.

3 When a new document is created from the template, the only item that can be changed is the page Title. Any other changes that are made will not take effect

Highlighting editable and locked regions

If there are a lot of editable regions within a template/ document, it can be easy to become confused as to what is editable and what is locked. To overcome this, specific colours can be assigned to both. However, when working with a template only the editable region colour is visible, and when working with a document based on a template, the locked region colour is also visible, as an outer border. To set colours for editable and locked regions:

1. In a template or a document based on a template, select Edit> Preferences from the menu bar

To view the highlight colours in a template and a document based on it, select View>Visual Aids>Invisible Elements from the menu bar.

2. Select Highlighting and click here to access the colour palettes for the Editable and Locked Regions

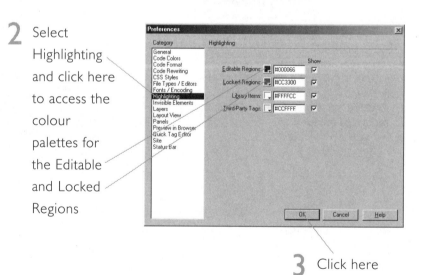

3. Click here

Creating pages from templates

Once templates have been created, it is then possible to produce new Web pages in Dreamweaver, based on these templates. To do this:

When templates are created, they are specific to the site in which they were produced. To use a template in another site, open it, select Save As Template from the menu bar and then, in the Save As Template dialog box, select the site in which you want the template to be available.

1 Select File>New from Template from the menu bar

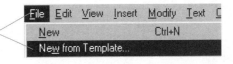

2 In the Select Template dialog box, select the site where the template is located and select the required template. Click on Select to have the template applied to the new document

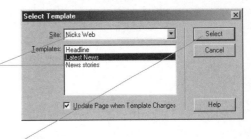

In a document based on a template, the outer border identifies the template on which the document is based and also the fact that everything within it is locked, unless it has been specified as an editable region.

3 A new HTML document is opened, based on the selected template. It is identified as a new document rather than a template as it does not have <<Template>> in the title

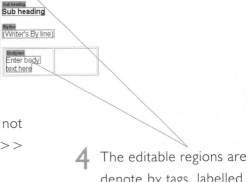

4 The editable regions are denote by tags, labelled with the region's name

Updating pages based on templates

If you have created several pages based on a single template, it is possible to update all of these pages by editing the template and applying these changes to all of the pages that have been created from it. This can be done as shown on page 65, or:

1 Open a page that is based on a template that has been created within the same site structure

2 Select Modify> Templates>Open Attached Template

If you check on the Show Log box in the Update Pages dialog box then a log will appear detailing all of the pages that have been updated.

3 Make the required editing changes to the template and select Modify>Templates> Update Pages from the menu bar

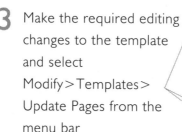

Once the template file has been updated, save it, so that the changes can then be applied to the relevant pages.

4 In the Update Pages dialog, select a site and click Start to update those pages based on the current template. Select Close to finish

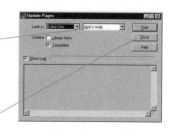

About the Library

During the design process of a Web site there will probably be some elements that you will want to reuse on different pages within the site. These could be static elements that appear on several pages, such as a company logo, or items where one part is updated regularly, such as a latest news section. Instead of having to create or insert these elements from their source location each time you want to use them, Dreamweaver has a facility for storing them and then dragging them onto a page whenever they are required. The location in which they are stored is known as the Library. Each site can have its own individual Library, with items that are used throughout that site.

When an item is placed in the Library it creates a Library item file that links to the source location in which that item is stored. So if the item is an image, there will be a link to its location on the hard drive. This means that the image can be reused numerous times without increasing the file size of the page. Rather than placing a copy of the item on a page each time it is taken from the Library, Dreamweaver creates a reference (or instance) back to the source location of the item. As long as the item is not moved from its source location then the Library version can be reused as many times as you like. Also, Library items can be updated, if required, and any changes made to them will be reflected in all of the instances of it in the site. To access the Library:

Click here on the Launcher palette and then click here on the Assets panel

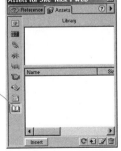

Creating Library items

Items can be added to the Library from any open Dreamweaver document. These will then be available in the Library to all other pages within that site. To add items to the Library:

Blocks of text and images can be converted into Library items, as can tables and forms and more complicated elements such as Flash movies.

Images can be selected by clicking on them once and text can be selected by dragging the cursor over the required section.

Items can also be added to the Library by selecting them and then selecting Modify>Library> Add Object to Library, or clicking on the New Library Item button on the Assets panel.

1 Open a file in the Design view and make sure the Library panel is visible, as shown on the previous page

Here is the latest breaking news:

2 Select the item that you want to include in the Library

Here is the latest breaking news:

3 Drag and drop the item into either panel of the Library

4 Type a name for the Library item

Adding items from the Library

Once items have been created in the Library, they can then be reused on any page within the site structure. To do this:

Library items are created as individual files with a '–.lib' extension.

To see the HTML code for Library items once they have been inserted into a document, select the HTML Source button on the Launcher palette.

Once a Library item has been added to a document, it will remain there even if it is then subsequently deleted from the Library.

To change the colour used to highlight Library items when they are placed in a document, select Edit>Preferences from the menu bar, select Highlighting as the category and select a colour from the box next to Library Items.

1 Select an item in the Library

2 Drag and drop the selected Library item onto the Design view page

OR

Click on the Insert button on the Library panel

3 An instance of the Library item is placed on the page. This is locked, i.e. it cannot be edited in Design view and is highlighted by the colour specified in the Highlighting section of the Preferences dialog box

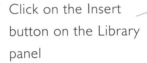

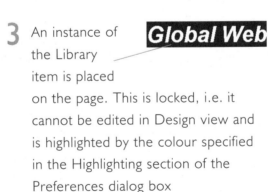

Editing Library items

Library items are very versatile in that it is possible to edit them in the Library itself, in which case the changes apply to all of the instances of these items throughout the site, or individual Library items in a document can be made editable so that they can then be edited independently.

When a Library item is opened, it is done so in a separate window, with a grey background and the words <<Library Item>> in the title.

Editing items in the Library

If you open and edit items in the Library itself, these changes can be applied to all occurrences of that item throughout a whole site. To do this:

A Library item can also be edited by clicking on the right pointing arrow at the top of the Assets panel and selecting Edit from the menu.

1 Open an item in the Library by double-clicking the name or by clicking the Edit button

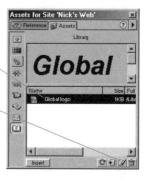

When a Library item is being edited, it appears on a grey background, as opposed to the standard white background in Design view.

2 In the Library Item window, make editing changes to the item. Select File>Save from the menu bar to apply the changes

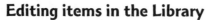

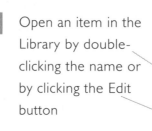

If you do not want to update all of the pages in which a Library item occurs, select Don't Update in the Update Library Items dialog box. If required this can be done at a later stage.

3 The Update Library Items dialog box will appear, asking if you want to update this item in all of the files in which it occurs. Select Update

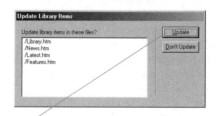

Editing Library items in a document

Once a Library item has been placed in a document it is still possible to perform certain editing tasks on it:

1 Select a Library item on a document page by clicking on it once. It will not be possible to edit this directly

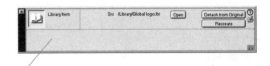

2 The Library properties box will be displayed

Click here to detach the item in the document from the source Library item. This means that it can be edited in the document window, but it will not have any changes applied to it if the source Library item is edited

If an instance of a Library item is detached from the source document, then it loses all of the attributes it had previously. It no longer functions as a Library item.

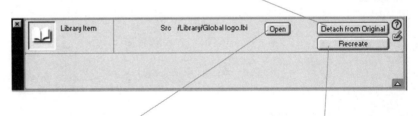

If a Library item is edited and you then want to update all of the pages that contain that item, make sure the Library Items box is checked on in the Update Pages dialog box.

Click here to open the item in the Library window. The content can then be edited

Click here to reinstate a Library item, if the original has been deleted from the Library palette

Creating editable navigation bars

If you have a site that contains a navigation bar on several hundred pages you will soon come to appreciate the importance of creating it as a Library item so that it can be updated site-wide in a single operation.

After updating a Library item, make sure that all of the relevant files are uploaded to the remote site i.e. the one that is visible to other users.

A Library item can also be edited by clicking here: and selecting Edit from the menu.

One of the most common reasons for updating navigation bars that have been converted to Library items is to amend the links within the bar.

A navigation bar is a set of buttons that can help the user navigate between the most commonly used areas or pages of a Web site. They can appear at the top or the side of all pages throughout a site. This has the advantage of creating a uniform style and it makes the user feel comfortable within the site. For information about creating navigation bars, see page 112. One of the possible drawbacks with navigation bars is that if you have them throughout your site and then decide to update a link within them, then it can be a laborious task. This can be greatly simplified by creating the navigation bar as a Library item:

1 Create a navigation bar and convert it into a Library item by dragging it into one of the Library panels

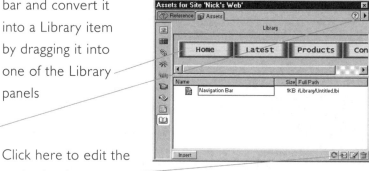

2 Click here to edit the navigation bar

3 Apply the editing changes and then select File>Save in the menu bar

4 You will be prompted as to whether you want to update all of the pages that contain this Library item. Select Update

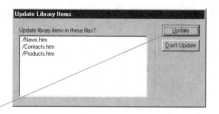

Adding text

This chapter looks at how to add text to Web pages and how to format its size and colour. It also shows how to apply emphasis to text, align it, indent it and produce lists.

Covers

Inserting text | 78

Text properties | 79

Fonts | 80

Size | 82

Colour | 84

Emphasis and alignment | 85

Lists | 86

Indents | 87

Copy and Paste | 88

Chapter Five

Inserting text

Although Web pages can contain an array of multimedia and graphical effects, text is still the most common way of conveying information on a Web site. Due to the formatting functions that are available in programs like Dreamweaver, it is possible to use text as not only a means of conveying information but also as a design tool in its own right.

When a new document is opened in Dreamweaver the cursor will already be inserted at the top left of the page. It will be flashing, indicating that it is ready to have text inserted at this point. To do this, just start typing as you would if you were using a word processing program:

Text can be deleted by selecting it and then pressing the back delete key. On a PC, text in front of the insertion point of the cursor can be removed by pressing the Delete key and text behind it can be removed by pressing the back delete key. On a Mac, only the back delete key is available.

Add text by typing at the point where the cursor is flashing

Click and start typing|

Make changes to existing text by inserting the cursor and adding or deleting text

Insert and ad| or delete

Highlight a single word by double-clicking on it. Highlight a block of text by inserting the cursor at the end of it and then selecting Shift+click at the beginning of it, or drag select it by holding down the mouse button and dragging the cursor over the required text.

Overwrite existing text by highlighting it and then typing the new text

Highlight to overwrite

Text properties

Whenever text is being added or edited, the Text Properties box is displayed. This shows the attributes of the current piece of text and it can be used to perform a variety of text formatting tasks:

If the Text Properties box is not showing when you insert or edit text, select Window> Properties from the menu bar.

Text format. Allows different styles to be applied to text

Font

Size

Colour

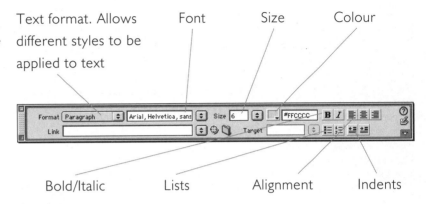

Bold/Italic

Lists

Alignment

Indents

A lot of these commands can also be selected from the menu bar:

The Text Properties box also has options for creating textual hyperlinks to other pages or Web sites. This is looked at in more detail in Chapter Seven.

Select Text from the menu bar and then the required item

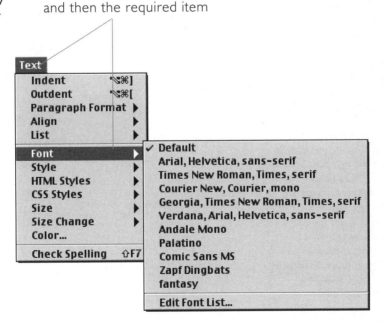

Fonts

There are literally hundreds of fonts available for use in creating Web pages. These range from the subdued and sombre to the weird and wacky. Generally, the fonts used on individual sites are in keeping with the content of the site: a Web site for a firm of solicitors would probably contain different fonts to that for a cutting-edge design firm or a company selling computer games. The important factor about using fonts is consistency: use the same fonts for body text, headings and sub-headings throughout your site.

Fonts can be applied to existing items of text by selecting them first, or a new font can be selected before you start inserting text. To select a font:

Do not clutter up your Web sites with dozens of different fonts, as this can become irritating for the user. Pick two or three fonts and then use them consistently throughout the site. This way, users will identify a certain font with a particular element of your site, such as a heading.

If you do not specify a font, Dreamweaver will use the Default Font. This can be specified by selecting Edit>Preferences from the menu bar and entering a font and size for the proportional font in the Font/Encoding window. However, this only applies to the default font in Dreamweaver: when it is viewed in a browser it will take on the attributes of the browser's default font, which will probably be something like Times Roman.

So it is possible that the text will be displayed in different fonts on different browsers if the default setting is applied.

Click here to access the standard Dreamweaver list of the most commonly used fonts. Each option has three or four possibilities, in case the user's computer does not have the first choice. Click on one to select it

The selected font will be applied to any highlighted text and also any text that is inserted subsequently

This is the selected font

Adding more fonts

There is no reason why you have to stick to list of standard Dreamweaver fonts and you can add fonts that are stored on your own hard drive or from a CD-ROM:

If you choose an unusual or obscure font the person viewing your page will not be able to see the selected font unless they have it installed on their own computer. This means the text will be displayed in a similar font, or the browser default. Either way, it could look dramatically different from how you intended.

1 Select Edit Font List to add fonts to the standard list

2 In the Edit Font List dialog box, click here to view the available fonts on your computer

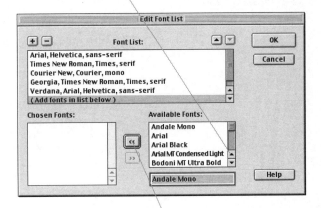

3 Click here to add a font to the Dreamweaver font list

4 The selected fonts are now available on the font list in the Text Properties box

Size

The size of text can have just as important an impact on a Web page as the font. If used consistently, different sizes of text can be used to easily identify body text and different types of headings. The size of text can be changed manually, or by using preset format styles:

Changing size manually

| Select a piece of text

Change the size

2 Click here in the Text Properties box to access the options for changing the size

3 Select a size for the text, ranging from 1 (smallest) to 7 (largest)

4 Click here to apply an incremental change to a piece of text (see the tip)

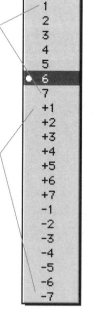

Using Styles

Text size and formatting can be specified using preset styles from either the Text Properties box or the Text>Format menu:

Formatting styles are applied to entire paragraphs i.e. all of the text between the <p></p> tags.

Once a formatting style has been applied, it is possible to apply further formatting to it, such as italics and alignment.

It is possible to create your own preset styles for formatting text, by using the HTML Styles palette. For more information on this see Chapter Eleven.

Heading styles will only take effect if a size for the text has not already been selected in the font size box.

1 Insert the cursor within a paragraph that you want to format

Paragraphs can have preformatted styles applied to them.

2 Click here on the Text Properties box to access the formatting options

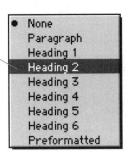

Format | None |
Link |

3 Select a formatting style. Heading 1 is the largest size of heading and Heading 6 is the smallest

• None
Paragraph
Heading 1
Heading 2
Heading 3
Heading 4
Heading 5
Heading 6
Preformatted

4 The selected style will be applied to the whole paragraph in which the cursor was inserted

Paragraphs can have preformatted styles applied to them.

Format | Heading 2 |
Link |

Colour

Colour is an excellent way to draw attention to text on a Web page. It can be used to highlight particular items or as a theme for consistent elements throughout a site. For instance, you could have all main headings in one colour and the body text in another. However, do not get too carried away with using too many different colours on a single page: instead of creating an eye-catching and dynamic design you may just end up with a distracting rainbow effect. To add colour to text:

Make sure that there is always a good contrast between text colour and the background on which it appears e.g. black text on a white background. If the text colour and the background are too similar, the text will be indistinct and difficult to read.

1 Select the section of text that you want to change the colour for

Select to change the colour

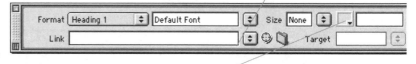

The background colour for a Web page can be set by selecting Modify>Page Properties from the menu bar and selecting a colour in the Background box.

2 Click here to access the text colour palette

3 Select a colour for the palette. This will be displayed as a hexadecimal value

A hexadecimal value is a six character code that is used to display colours by defining how much red, green and blue they have. Hexadecimal values use numbers from 1–9 and letters from A–F.

4 The selected colour is displayed here and its hexadecimal value is displayed here

Emphasis and alignment

Two further ways of formatting text are adding bold and italics for emphasis and adjusting the alignment on the page.

Bold and italics

Bold and italics can also be applied by selecting a piece of text and pressing Ctrl+B (Windows) or Command+B (Mac) and Ctrl+I (Windows) or Command+I (Mac) respectively.

❙ Select a piece of text

Select to make **bold and italic**

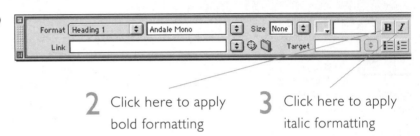

2 Click here to apply bold formatting

3 Click here to apply italic formatting

Alignment

❙ Select a piece of text

2 Click here to left align the text

Text can be aligned with even greater precision through the use of tables. The text can be placed within the cells of a table and then have the alignment functions listed here applied to it.

Select to align left, right or centre

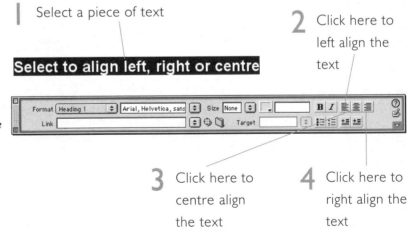

3 Click here to centre align the text

4 Click here to right align the text

Lists

There are functions for producing bulleted and numbered lists and also for indenting lines or paragraphs of text.

Lists

Lists can be used to break up long passages of text, or convey complicated arguments more clearly. Bulleted lists should be used if all of the points are of equal importance, while numbered lists can be used for items of varying importance.

	Select a piece of text

2 Click here to create a bulleted list ————

3 Click here to create a numbered list ————

Further list formatting options

	Select part of a list —

2 Click on the List Item button in the properties box

3 Select the options in the List Properties dialog box

Indents

The indenting option can be used to move text to the left or the right and also create nested lists i.e. lists within lists:

I Select a piece of text

Text can be

indented

quickly and easily

Indenting is not always an exact science in HTML and it can be easier to move text by using the Spacebar or inserting a non-breaking space.

2 Click here to right indent the text

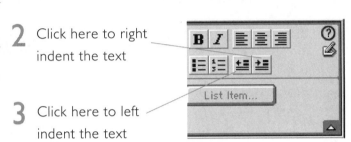

3 Click here to left indent the text

Creating nested lists

Left indents can only be used if an item has already been right indented.

I Select part of an existing list or insert the cursor

For my Web site I need:
- A designer
- A| server
- Dreamweaver

2 Click on the right indent button to nest the list to the next level

For my Web site I need:
- A designer
  - o A server
- Dreamweaver

Indents are denoted in the HTML source code with the <blockquote></blockquote> tags.

3 Repeat the process if any further levels of nesting are required

For my Web site I need:
- A designer
    - □ A| server
- Dreamweaver

Copy and Paste

Dreamweaver employs the standard copy and paste techniques used in most word processing and desktop publishing programs. In addition, it also has a function for copying HTML code from other applications and then pasting the code into a Dreamweaver document.

Basic Copy and Paste

To copy (or cut) text from one location in a Dreamweaver document and insert it in another document:

If you select a piece of text and select Copy, it is placed on the clipboard ready to be pasted, while the original text is left in place. If you select Cut then the original piece of text is removed.

1 Select a piece of text —— Select text to be copied

2 Select Edit>Copy (or Cut) from the menu bar

Edit	
Undo Typing	⌘Z
Repeat Typing	⌘Y
Cut	⌘X
Copy	⌘C

3 Insert the cursor where you want the text to appear and select Edit>Paste from the menu bar

Edit	
Undo Typing	⌘Z
Repeat Typing	⌘Y
Cut	⌘X
Copy	⌘C
Paste	⌘V

Using Paste as HTML

To copy HTML from another application and paste it into Code view in Dreamweaver:

1 Select and copy a piece of HTML code from another application

2 Insert the cursor where you want the new code and Select Edit>Paste as HTML from the menu bar

Working with images

Images can be a powerful design tool on a Web page, as long as they are used economically and effectively. This chapter gives an overview of using images on the Web and explains how to insert and edit them in Dreamweaver. It also shows how to create rollover images.

Covers

Web image overview | 90

Using images effectively | 91

Inserting images | 92

Image properties | 93

Resizing images | 94

Aligning images and text | 95

Creating rollover images | 97

Chapter Six

Web image overview

When the Web was first being developed it was considered to be a significant achievement to transfer plain, unformatted, text from one computer to another. However, things have moved on considerably from then and the Web is now awash with complex graphics, animations and sounds, to name but a few of the multimedia effects that are now available to the Web designer.

Despite the range of items that can be used on Web pages, graphics are still by far the most popular. These can include photographic images, icons, clip art and even animated graphics. These are all important design elements for Web pages and they should not be overlooked when you are creating a new Web site.

There are other image formats for use on the Web, such as Portable Network Group (PNG), but GIFs and JPEGs are by far the most common.

When graphical formats were being developed for the Web there was a need to create good quality images that were still small enough to allow them to be downloaded quickly onto the user's computer. This resulted in two file formats that offer good quality while still creating small file sizes. These are Graphical Interchange Format (GIF) and Joint Photographic Experts Group (JPEG). Some points to bear in mind about both of these formats:

- JPEGs use up to 16 million colours and so are best suited for photographic images

If you use an image editing program, such as Macromedia Fireworks, images can be optimised so that the best quality can be matched with the smallest file size.

- GIFs use 256 colours and so are best suited for images that do not contain a lot of colour definition, such as images with blocks of similar colour

- One variety of GIF (GIF 89a) can be used to create images with transparent backgrounds

- Both GIFs and JPEGs use forms of compression to make the file size smaller

Using images effectively

When you use a program such as Dreamweaver, which gives you the power to quickly and easily insert images into Web pages, the temptation is to add them at every opportunity. However, this should be resisted as it is important to use images carefully and make the most of their impact and design potential. Some points to bear in mind when using images on Web pages are:

Do not make your Web site too dependant on images, since users can set their browsers so that they do not display any graphics.

- The more images you include, the longer it will take for the user to download your site i.e. access it from the host server. This can cause a real problem, because most Web users do not have the patience to wait a long time for pages to download. This can be measured in seconds rather than minutes

- Images can be used as the background to a Web page or as independent items within it. Either way, the file size of the image will determine the downloading time

- Keep the onscreen size of images small. Again, this can affect the downloading time and it can detract from other content on a page

- Do not overuse images that spin, blink or flicker. While this can create a positive initial effect, it can become extremely irritating after it has been viewed several times

Always try and use a textual Alt tag to describe an attached image. This can be useful for people who have selected not to view images, and also visually impaired people who view Web pages with a device that reads the content from the screen.

- Use images for a specific purpose, i.e. to convey information or as a design feature

- Do not use images that could be deemed offensive or derogatory to any individuals or groups

- Use the same image, or groups of images, to achieve a consistent look throughout a Web site

Inserting images

Obtaining images

Images for insertion in a Web site can be obtained from a variety of sources:

- System clip art collections (most computers come with some items of clip art already pre-installed)

- CD-ROMs. There are several CD-ROMs on the market that contain tens of thousands of graphical and photographic images

- Digital cameras. These are affordable for the home user and offer a versatile option for creating your own images for a Web page

- Scanners. These can be used to capture existing images in a digital format

For a detailed look at digital cameras and digital images, take a look at 'Digital Photography in easy steps'.

Inserting images

To use an image for the background of a page, select Modify>Page Properties from the menu bar. Click on the Browse button next to the Background Image box and select an image in the same way as for inserting it directly onto a page.

To create a watermark effect, use an image editing program to make the image semi-transparent and then insert it as the background.

1 Insert the cursor at the point on the page where you want the image and click on the Insert Image button in the Common panel of the Objects palette

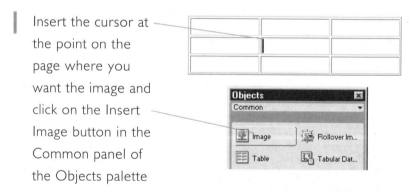

2 Locate the image you want to use and click on Select (Windows) or Choose (Mac)

Image properties

When an image is selected in Dreamweaver, the properties box displays information about that image. To access the image properties box:

When an image is inserted on a page in Dreamweaver, this is only really a reference to where the image is physically located on your computer, rather than the image itself being physically inserted. This is denoted by the <src> tag.

| Select an image by clicking on it once

Using Alternative (Alt) text in place of an image is important for people who choose not to view images or who are visually impaired and use a reader to view the Web. Type a description of the image in the Alt box. This can be a couple of words or several sentences.

2 The image properties box is activated. Click here to expand it to view all of the options

File details and image name

Image dimensions

Image location

Alignment and alternative text

By using image maps it is possible to places several hyperlinks to other pages, within a single image. For more on this, see Chapter Seven.

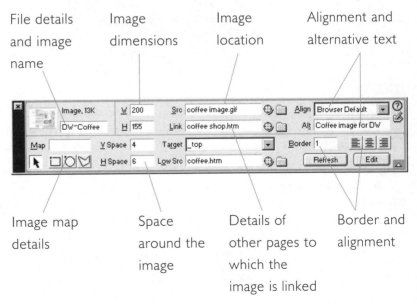

Image map details

Space around the image

Details of other pages to which the image is linked

Border and alignment

Resizing images

Even if you have sized an image in an image editing program before it is inserted into a Dreamweaver document, there is a good chance that it will not be exactly the right size for your purposes. To resize an image:

The image properties box will be activated automatically when an image is selected.

To change the horizontal and vertical size of an image proportionally, hold down shift while you are dragging the corner resizing button.

Do not resize images too many times, or else the image quality will deteriorate.
The quality will be better if you decrease the size of the image rather than increase it.

| Select an image by clicking on it once

2 Click here to change the horizontal or vertical size

3 Click here to change the horizontal and vertical size simultaneously

4 Instead of step 3, enter values in the image properties box to alter the height and width of the image

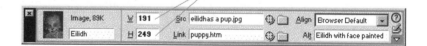

Aligning images and text

During the process of creating a Web site, there will several occasions where you will want to combine images and text. This could be to include a textual definition of an image or to wrap a block of text around an image, in the style of a newspaper or a magazine article. This can be done through the use of various Dreamweaver functions (see tip) or an image can have a value assigned to it so that it deals with text alignment in a certain way. To align an image and text together:

One of the most versatile ways of aligning and laying out images and text is through the use of tables. This will enable you to produce precision alignment. The alignment options on this page can also be applied to images and text once they are inserted into a table. For more on tables, see Chapter Eight.

Layers in Dreamweaver can also be used to align images and text. For more on layers, see Chapter Nine.

1 Select an image by clicking on it once. It can already have text around it, or the text can be added later

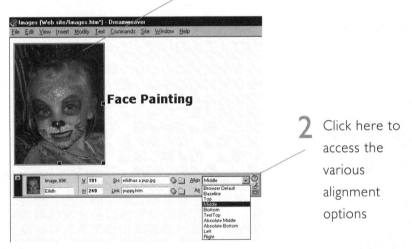

2 Click here to access the various alignment options

The baseline of a text block is the line on which the bottom of most of the letters sit. This does not include descenders (such as g and j) which extend below the baseline.

The options for aligning images and text are:

- Browser default. This varies with browsers but it usually aligns the text baseline with the image base

- Baseline. This aligns the baseline with the image base

- Top. This aligns the tallest point of the text with the top of the image

- Middle. This aligns the text baseline with the middle of the image

- Bottom. This aligns the baseline of the text with the bottom of the image

- Text Top. This aligns the tallest point of the text with the top of the image

- Absolute Middle. This aligns the middle of the text block with the middle of the image

- Absolute Bottom. This aligns the bottom of the text, including descenders, with the bottom of the image

- Left. This places the image to the left of any text that is next to it. The text will then wrap around the image

- Right. This places the image to the right of any text that is next to it

Aligning images and text can create some interesting, and sometimes unwanted, effects. Experiment with different settings until you feel confident about each combination.

Alignment buttons

As well as using the alignment options described above, it is also possible to align images and text by using the alignment buttons in the image properties box. Even though this is done by selecting an image, the alignment is applied to the text:

Another use for images is the Trace option. This is where a design has been created and is then inserted onto a Web page as a background for the Web designer to copy, or trace over. The trace image does not appear on the published page and it is really a guide for the Web designer to follow.

To use a trace image, select Modify>Page Properties from the menu bar and in the Tracing Image box select the trace image as you would for any other image. There are also options for applying certain levels of transparency.

1 This is an example of an image with the left alignment option and the left align button:

2 This is an example of an image with the middle alignment option and the centre align button:

Creating rollover images

One of the most eye-catching effects with images on the Web is the creation of rollovers. This is where two images are combined, although only one is visible initially on the page. However, when the cursor is moved over the image, it is replaced by the second one. To make this even more impressive, a hyperlink can be added to the rollover so that the user can click on it and they will be taken to another page within the site, or a different site altogether.

Do not get too carried away with using rollovers, although this can be difficult to resist when you first learn how to create them. As with any item on a Web page that moves or changes from one thing to another, a little goes a long way.

Until recently, rollovers were the preserve of designers who could use programming languages such as Javascript. However, Dreamweaver overcomes this by allowing you to create rollovers, while generating all of the script in the background. This means that you have a powerful design tool at your disposal, without having to delve into computer language scripting.

Creating a rollover image

1 Create the two images that you want to use for the rollover. Make sure they are approximately the same dimensions because they will be produced as the same size in the rollover

If you are using a rollover to link to another page or site on the Web, choose your images carefully so that the user can quickly relate the image with the link that it contains. Otherwise, they may think that it is just a clever graphical effect.

2 Insert the cursor where you want the rollover to appear and click the Rollover Image button on the common pane of the Objects palette

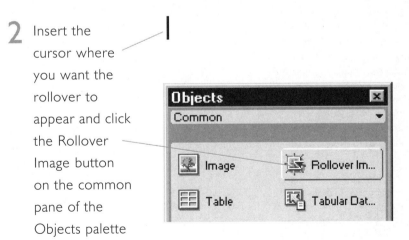

3 Click here to enter a name for the rollover button

One effective device is to use the same image for both the initial image and the rollover one. However, edit the rollover image to be a different colour, or some degree of transparency. This will then produce a subtle effect when the rollover is activated.

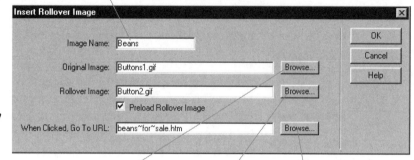

Insert Rollover Image

Image Name:	Beans
Original Image:	Buttons1.gif	Browse...
Rollover Image:	Button2.gif	Browse...
	☑ Preload Rollover Image
When Clicked, Go To URL:	beans~for~sale.htm	Browse...

OK
Cancel
Help

URL stands for Uniform Resource Locator and it is a unique address for every page on the Web. It is usually in a format similar to 'www.mysite.com'

If you are linking to a page on your own site, you only need to insert the page name i.e. news.htm. But if you want to link to an external Web site, you will need to insert the full URL, which can be copied from the address bar in the browser when you are viewing the page.

4 Click here to locate the first image you are going to use. Repeat the process by clicking here for the second image

5 If you want the user to be able to go to another Web page when they click, click here to select a page to link to. Click OK to create the rollover

To test a rollover, save the file and press F12 or select File>Preview in Browser from the menu bar.

Using hyperlinks

This chapter looks at how items on Web pages can be linked together through the use of hyperlinks. It shows how to create links to other Web pages and also to items within the same page. It also demonstrates how to create image maps and navigation bars.

Covers

About hyperlinks | 100

Linking to documents | 103

Linking to anchors | 105

Creating an email link | 107

Point-to-file links | 108

Image maps | 111

Navigation bars | 112

Chapter Seven

About hyperlinks

Without hyperlinks (or just links), the Web would be an unconnected collection of pages and sites that would be tortuous to navigate around since you would have to specify the Web address (URL) for each page that you wanted to view. Hyperlinks simplify this process considerably: they are pieces of HTML coding that create 'clickable' regions on a Web page i.e. the user can click on a hyperlink and it will take them to the linked item. In simple terms, hyperlinks are shortcuts for jumping between elements on the Web.

URL stands for Uniform Resource Locator and it refers to the unique address of every page on the Web.

Both text and images can be used as hyperlinks: text usually appears underlined when it is acting as a hyperlink and, for both elements, the cursor turns into a pointing hand when it is positioned over a hyperlink on a Web page. If you click at this point you will be taken to the linked item. Some of the items that hyperlinks can be linked to are:

If you are using images as hyperlinks, make sure that they are clearly identifiable, otherwise the user may think they are just a graphical design feature.

- Other pages within the same Web site

- Other locations within the same page

- Other Web sites

- Email addresses

Hyperlinks to other Web pages are created by using the <a href= > tag, which is closed by inserting the </a> tag. So the code for a simple hyperlink to a page within the same site structure could look like:

<a href="news.htm">Latest News</a>

In this example the words 'Latest News' would be underlined on the page and when the user clicks on them, the page 'news.htm' will open.

Document-relative links

Depending on the type of link that is being created, the address that you use as the link will vary. For instance, if you are linking to a page within your own site, this is called a document-relative link and if you are linking to another site on the Web, this is called an absolute link.

A document-relative link to a file within the same structure and in the same folder would have a link straight to the file name i.e. <a href="main.htm">My Day</a>. This is the simplest type of link to insert and, if possible, it is preferable to try and use this format as much as possible.

If you want to link to a file in a sub-folder of the one in which your source folder is located, then the link would look like this:

<a href="events/main.htm">My Day</a>

Always save files within a site structure before you add hyperlinks. This way, Dreamweaver will have a reference point for where the links are going from. This is particularly important for when the site is published on the Web.

If these two files were linked, the hyperlink code would be as above

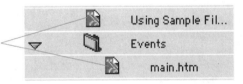

If you want to link to a file in the main (or parent) folder to the one in which your source folder is located, then the link would look like this:

<a href="../birthday.htm">Celebrate</a>

The notation '../' in a hyperlink address means move up one level in the folder hierarchy and '/' means move down one level. This acts as an instruction to the browser viewing a page as to where to look for the linked file.

If your site structure consists of several different levels of folders, your links can become quite complicated. Luckily, Dreamweaver takes care of making sure the correct notation is inserted.

If these two files were linked, the hyperlink code would be as above

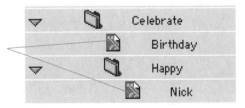

Absolute links

An absolute link is one that goes externally to another page on the Web i.e. one that is stored on another server. This means that the full URL has to be inserted so the browser viewing the pages knows where to look. An absolute path for a Web page is always prefixed with 'http://' and then followed by the address of the page. So the absolute link to the Dreamweaver page on the Macromedia Web site would be:

http://www.macromedia.com/software/dreamweaver/

In some cases the file extension will have to be added at the end of the URL, but in others it will be set up so that the full URL does not have to be entered because the '/' at the end instructs the browser to look for the associated index page.

Email links

As well as being able to link to Web pages, hyperlinks can also be used to take the user to a specific email address, where they can compose and send a message. This is a created with the following code as the link:

<a href="mailto: nickvandome@hotmail.com">Nick Vandome</a>

It is also possible to create a link to an external page on the Web by manually typing in the absolute path of the page to which you want to link. However, it is better to visit the target page on the Web, copy its URL from the address bar at the top of the browser and then paste this as your link in Dreamweaver.

When an email link is activated, the user's email program will open up, with the recipient's name already inserted in the To box of a new mail message

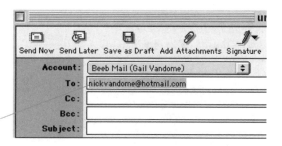

Linking to documents

Links can be created to a variety of documents, including images, sounds and videos clips, but the most common type of link is to another Web page. Dreamweaver provides a number of ways to achieve this:

Using the Properties Inspector

1 Select an image or piece of text which you want to make into a link

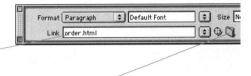

2 Click here and enter the URL of the page to which you want to link

OR

Click here to browse your hard drive for a file to link to. Once you have chosen one, click on Select (Windows) or Choose (Mac)

If you browse to a file outside your current site structure, and try and link to it, a warning box will appear alerting you to the fact that the file is not contained within the current structure. You will be given the option of then saving it within the current structure. This will be beneficial for the linking process.

3 The selected file will now be visible here:

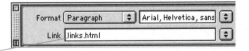

Using the menu bar

1 Select an image or piece of text which you want to make into a link

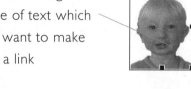

2 Select Modify>Make Link from the menu bar and select a file as shown on the previous page

Using the contextual menu

1 Select an image or piece of text which you want to make into a link

2 Right-click (Windows) or Ctrl+click (Mac) and select Make Link from the contextual menu that appears. Select a file as shown on the previous page

Linking to anchors

As well as being able to create hyperlinks to other pages within your own site, and external sites, it is also possible to use links to move about the same page. This can be particularly useful if you have a lot of text on a page, or several sections, and you want to enable the users to navigate around the page without having to scroll down the page too much. In Dreamweaver this is done through the use of anchors. These are inserted on the page at the required points and hyperlinks are then created to them from other parts of the page. To do this:

Anchors are also known as bookmarks in other Web authoring programs.

It is not necessary to select an image or a piece of text when creating an anchor. The anchor is independent of any other item on the page and is placed at the insertion point of the cursor.

When naming anchors, give them a single name. It is possible to enter more than one name in the dialog box, but this can cause problems when the link is trying to find the specified anchor.

1 Insert the cursor at the point where you want the anchor to appear

2 Select Insert>Invisible Tags>Named Anchor from the menu bar

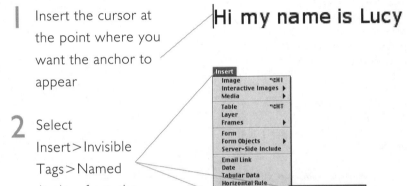

3 In the Insert Named Anchor dialog box, type a name for the anchor. This is the name that will be used in the hyperlink to the anchor. Select OK

4 The anchor will be denoted on the page by the following element. Click on it to see the anchor's properties

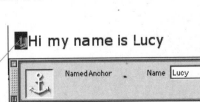

5 Select the image or piece of text on the page that is going to act as the link to the named anchor. This is frequently an item at the top of the page

All about us

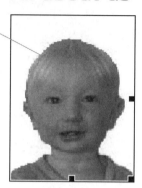

Lucy

If you are using a lot of anchors on a page, it is advisable to include a link back to the top of the page at regular intervals, next to selected anchors. This means that the user will always have the means to quickly jump back to the top of the page rather than feeling lost in the middle of a long document.

To include a link back to the beginning of a document, insert an anchor at the top of the page and name it Top. Then move further down the document and type Top or Top of Page. Select the text and create a hyperlink to #top. When clicked, this should then take the user to the Top anchor at the beginning of the document.

6 In the Properties Inspector, enter the name of the anchor here, preceded by the # symbol

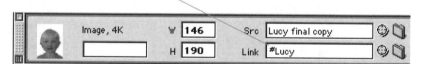

7 It is also possible to link to an anchor in another document, in which case the full filename should be inserted here, followed by # and the anchor name as above

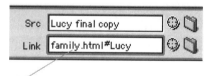

Press F12 or select File>Preview in Browser to test the page in a browser and make sure that the link goes to the correct anchor.

Creating an email link

To create a link that allows the user to access an email address, first insert the cursor at the point where you want the link to appear, then:

1 Click on the E-mail Link button in the Common panel of the Objects palette

If you include an email link on your site, it is a good idea to include some form of privacy statement, saying that you will not pass on any email addresses that you receive as a result of a message that you receive. Unfortunately, there are some unscrupulous individuals who do this sort of thing, resulting in the recipient being deluged with junk email.

2 In the Insert E-Mail Link dialog box, insert the text that will be displayed for the link and enter

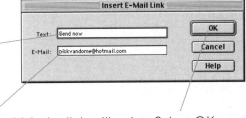

the email address to which the link will point. Select OK

3 The linked text will appear on the page and when it is selected the email address to which it is linked

Send now

will be shown in the Properties Inspector. When the link is activated, the user's email program will open, with the address pre-inserted in the To box

Point-to-file links

When you are creating links, there may be times when you do not want to insert the filename of the document to which you want to link, but rather just point to a file and instruct Dreamweaver to link to that item. With the innovative point-to-file tool you can do just that. Dreamweaver even lets you use it in several different ways.

Point-to-file in the document window

The point-to-file tool can be used to link two files that have both been opened in the document window:

The point-to-file technique cannot be used to create links to external Web pages, even if they are opened next to the document window.

1 Resize the two open files so that they are both visible in the document window

2 Select the image or piece of text which you want to use as the link

There is no command for tiling open files in Dreamweaver, so if you want to view two side-by-side they have to be resized by dragging the bottom right-corner and then positioning them accordingly on the screen.

3 Click here in the Properties Inspector and drag the cursor in to the file to be linked to

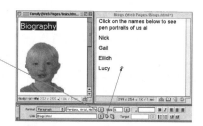

4 The item selected in Step 2 is now linked to the other document

Point-to-file in the site window

1 Select Window>
Site Map from the
menu bar

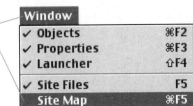

*If you want to
link a lot of
different files,
doing so with
the point-to-file
tool in the site window could
be the quickest way.
However, it would be
advisable to draw out a
rough sketch of how you
want the linked structure to
look.*

2 Select a file in the
Site Navigation
window

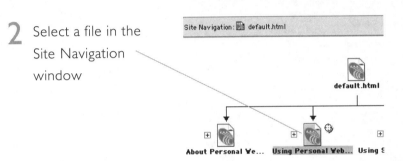

3 Click on this
icon and
drag to one
of the files
in the Local
Folder list

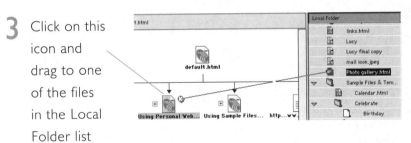

*The link that is
inserted into
the target file is
a plain text
one, consisting
of the page's filename. This
can be edited by opening the
file in a document window.*

4 A textual link will
automatically be
inserted in the file the
point-to-file link was
dragged from

Photo gallery

Point-to-file for anchors

1 Insert an anchor and select an item that is going to link to it

2 Hold down Shift and drag the cursor from the selected item to the anchor. An arrow will appear as you drag

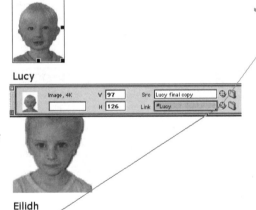

Lucy

Eilidh

3 Alternatively, click here and drag until the arrow is positioned over the anchor, then release

4 The link will have been made to the named anchor

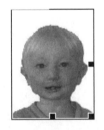

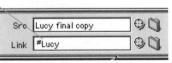

Image maps

An image map is a device that allows you to insert links to multiple files within a single image. As the name suggests this is ideal for geographical maps, where each location can be linked to a separate file, but it can also be used with any image that has easily identifiable areas. To create an image map:

1 Insert the image that is going to serve as the image map and select it by clicking on it once

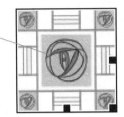

2 In the Properties Inspector, click on one of the hotspot tools

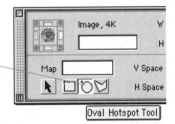

3 Draw an area on the image that is going to act as a hotspot. This is the area which the user will be able to click on and jump to the linked file

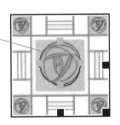

4 After a hotspot has been drawn, enter a file to link to here, or browse to select a file from your hard drive

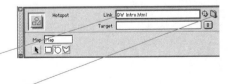

Navigation bars

One of the best devices for moving around a Web site is a navigation bar. This is a set of buttons that contain links to the other main areas of the site. Once a navigation bar has been created, it can be stored and placed on as many pages as required.

When a navigation bar is created, each button can have a different image assigned to it depending on its state i.e. how it is interacting with the cursor (see tip). To create a navigation bar:

Each button on a navigation bar can have four different states, made up of separate images:

- Up. This is the state when the button is inactive
- Over. This is the state when the cursor is passed over the button
- Down. This is the state when the button is pressed
- Over While Down. This is the state after the button has been released

1 Create the images that you want to use for the various states of the buttons in the navigation bar and click Navigation Bar in the Common panel of the Objects palette

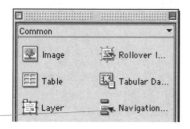

2 Name the first element of the navigation bar

Click here to add each button to the navigation bar. Repeat Steps 2–4 for each button you want to include on the navigation bar.

Each individual page can only have one navigation bar on it. In general, it is best to use the same navigation bar for a complete site.

3 Click here to select the images that are going to be used for each state of the button

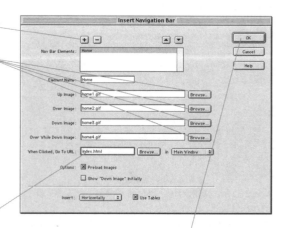

4 Click here to enter the page to which the button will link

5 Select OK

Tables and Layout view

This chapter shows how tables can be used to format the content of Web pages. It explains how to create tables, edit and format them and also how to add content and even create tables within tables. It also explains how Layout view can be used with tables to create complex layouts that will appear consistent in all browsers.

Covers

Designing with tables | 114

Inserting a table | 115

Editing a table | 117

Adding and deleting rows and columns | 119

Selecting cells | 120

Adding content | 122

Aligning items in a table | 123

Creating nested tables | 124

Layout view | 125

Chapter Eight

Designing with tables

One of the biggest challenges for any Web designer is to create a page layout that is both versatile and visually appealing. This invariably involves combining text and images and, before the advent of tables in HTML, it was a considerable problem trying to get everything in the right place. Even when elements looked correct on the designer's computer, there was no guarantee that they would appear the same when viewed on different computers and with different browsers. However, tables changed all that.

HTML tables are one of the most important design tools that are available to Web authors. Although their name suggests that they should perhaps only mainly be used to collate and display figures, this is definitely not the case: tables can contain the same content that is placed at any other point on an HTML page. They can then be used to position different elements and, since each item can be placed in its own individual cell within the table, the designer can be confident that this is the position in which they will appear, regardless of the browser used.

Tables can be used for simple formatting techniques, such as aligning text and images, or they can be used to display a whole page of complex design:

HTML tables are made up of a grid for the whole table, into which are placed rows and cells. The HTML code for these is:

- *Table — <table></table>*
- *Row — <tr></tr>*
- *Cell — <td></td>*

If the borders of a table are made invisible, i.e. set to 0, the user will not be aware that the content on the page is inside a table. This can make complex designs look even more impressive.

Inserting a table

You can insert as many tables as you like on a page and tables can also be nested i.e. tables placed within other tables. This provides even more versatility in the design process. When a table is inserted, various attributes can be set initially. However, it is also possible to edit and amend a table's attributes at any time after it has been created. To insert a table:

Tables can also be created by selecting Insert>Table from the menu bar. This brings up the same dialog box as using the Objects palette.

1 Click on the Table button in the Common panel of the Objects palette

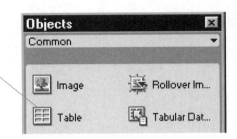

2 Enter the number of rows and columns that are required for the table

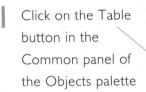

Use the percentage setting for the width of a table if you want to make sure it will all fit in the user's browser. However this could affect the way some of the content is displayed within the table. Use the pixel setting if you want the formatting to remain exactly as it has been designed.

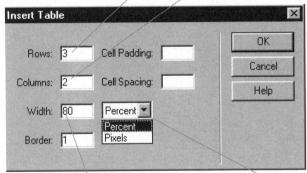

3 Enter a value for the size of the table. Click here to select a percentage size or a pixel size. If it is a percentage size, this will always appear as a percentage of the browser window in which it is being viewed. The pixel size is the actual physical size of the table

4 Enter a size for the table border. A value of 0 will create an invisible border and the default value is 1

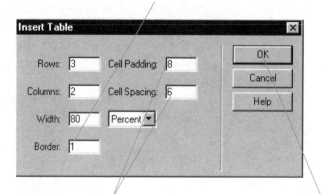

5 Enter values for the Cell Padding and the Cell Spacing. Cell padding affects how much space there is around each item in a cell and cell spacing affects how much space there is between the cells in a table

6 Click OK to create the table

If the cell padding is increased, the size of the individual cells increases too, since the area for adding content in the cell is still the same, it is just the area around it that increases. If the cell spacing is increased the size of the cells decreases, to accommodate the space around them.

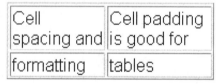

A table with cell padding and cell spacing both at 1

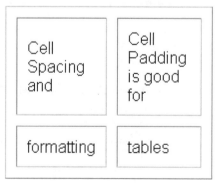

A table with cell padding and cell spacing both at 10

Editing a table

If you create a table and then decide you want to change some of its attributes, then it is possible to do so through the Properties Inspector. In addition to the settings that can be used in the Insert Table dialog box, there are also some additional attributes that can be used:

The resizing handles which appear when a table is selected can be used to change the dimensions of the table by dragging. The handle on the bottom resizes the table vertically, the one on the right side resizes it horizontally and the one in the right-corner resizes it both vertically and horizontally. Hold down Shift while dragging this button to change the dimensions proportionally.

1 Click once on a table's bottom or right border, or the top left corner to select it. A thick black line with 3 resizing handles should appear around it

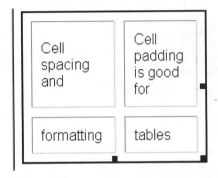

2 Once a table is selected the Table Properties Inspector will appear:

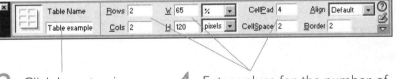

3 Click here to give the table a name

4 Enter values for the number of rows and columns, width and height and cell padding and cell spacing, in the same way as when the table was created

It is not essential to name tables, but it is a good way to keep track of them if you are using a lot that contain similar items of information.

5 Click here to access options for aligning the table on the page: this can be Left, Center or Right

If you select an image as the background for a table, make sure it does not detract from the content of the table itself.

7 Clear cell height or width

6 Click here to access additional table properties

Pixels can be used if you want to create a fixed-width table, i.e. one where the content retains its format whatever the size of the window in which it is being viewed. Depending on the design, this can result in the user having to scroll left and right to see the whole page.

Percent can be used if you want the table to always take up a certain portion of the screen. This can result in the content on the page becoming distorted from the original design.

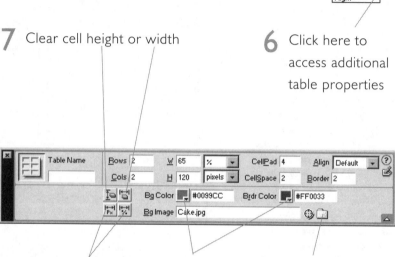

8 Change the table to pixels or percent

9 Click here to select a background colour for the table (left box) and an outer border colour (right box)

10 Click here to select an image for the table background

If colours for the Light and Dark borders are both selected, then any colour selected for the outer border of the table will not be applied.

Adding and deleting rows and columns

When tables are being used, particularly for complex designs, it is unlikely that the correct number of rows and columns will be specified first time. As shown on page 118, it is possible to add or delete the number of rows and columns by selecting the table and amending the values in the table Properties Inspector. This can also be achieved as follows:

To insert a single row or column, follow steps 1-2. To insert multiple rows or columns, follow steps 1 and 3-4.

Rows and columns can also be inserted or deleted by inserting the cursor in the table (but not selecting the table) and selecting Modify>Table from the menu bar. The same menu as in step 2 will appear.

Rows and columns can be resized by following steps 1 and 2 and then selecting Increase Row Span, Increase Column Span, Decrease Row Span or Decrease Column Span. They can also be resized by dragging the relevant row or column border.

1 Insert the cursor in the table where you want to add or delete rows or columns. Right-click (Windows) or Ctrl+click (Mac) and select Table

3 To insert multiple rows or columns, click Insert Rows or Columns

2 Insert a single row or column by selecting Insert Row or Insert Column. Delete one row or column by selecting Delete Row or Delete Column

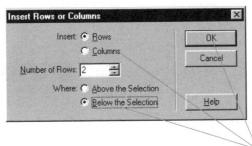

4 Enter whether you want to insert rows or columns, the number to be inserted and where you want them placed in relation to the insertion point. Click OK to insert the specified number of rows or columns

Selecting cells

If the cell you are trying to select is in the first column of a table, you have to drag the cursor to the right hand border of the cell. If it is in the last column of a table, you have to drag the cursor to the left hand border of the cell. If the cell you are trying to select is in any other column in the table, it can be selected by dragging the cursor to the left or right hand border. The same applies for selecting a cell within rows in a table.

Once a table has been created it can be useful to select individual cells, or groups of cells, so that specific formatting options can be applied to them. For instance, you may want to have a table where the top row of cells is a different size or colour to the rest of the cells in the table. Or you may want to apply separate formatting options to single cells.

Selecting cells

Insert the cursor in the cell you want to select, hold and drag to the outer border of the cell. A thick dark line appears around the cell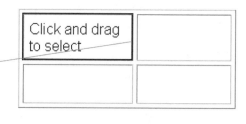

to indicate it has been selected. To select more than one cell, keep dragging until all of the required cells have been covered

Entire rows and columns can be selected by positioning the cursor on the relevant border until a thick black arrow appears and clicking once.

Merging cells

Once cells have been selected, it is then possible to merge them together, independently of the other cells in the table. This is an excellent formatting device as it allows the designer to break the symmetrical pattern of a table, which gives them increased flexibility. To merge cells once they have been selected:

Cells can also be merged by selecting them and then selecting Modify>Table>Merge Cells from the menu bar

1. With the required cells selected, right-click (Windows) or Ctrl+click (Mac) and select Table>Merge Cells

2. Or click here on the Properties Inspector

3 The selected cells
are now merged
independently of
the other cells in
the table

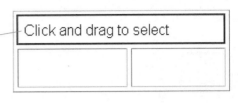

Splitting cells

Any cell within a table can be split into smaller parts,
regardless of whether it has already been merged or not. To
do this:

I Insert the cursor in
the cell you want to
split

*The Split Cell
option is only
available if you
select a single
cell. If you try
and activate this command
when more than one cell is
selected it will be greyed out
i.e. unavailable.*

2 Right-click
(Windows) or Ctrl+click
(Mac) and select
Table>Split Cell from the contextual menu

3 Or click here on the Properties
Inspector

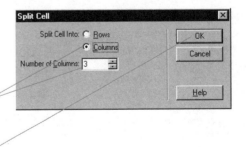

4 In the Split Cell
dialog box, select
whether you want to
split the cell into
rows and columns
and the required
number. Select OK

*If you split a
cell that
contains
content i.e. text
or images, this
will be placed in the left
hand cell if the cell is split
by columns, and the top cell
if it is split by rows.*

Adding content

If an item can be added to a page within Dreamweaver, then it can be inserted in a table too. A table acts only as a placeholder for content; it does not determine the type of content which it can display.

If you are including text and images in the same cell, insert a paragraph break <p></p> between them. This will make it possible to align them independently of each other, if required.

Adding text

1 Insert the cursor in the cell in which you want to include the text

If you are including text and images in the same cell, make sure the No Wrap option is not checked on. Otherwise the text will continue to fill the cell, and keep expanding it, rather than move onto the next line.

2 Enter the text and click on these buttons in the Properties Inspector to align it

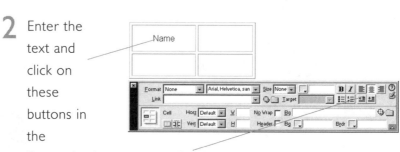

Adding images and more

Images, and any other form of multimedia content, can also be added to a table:

If you want to use a piece of text as the header for a table, select the Header option in the table properties box. This will embolden the text and centre it in the cell.

1 Insert the cursor in the cell in which you want the image or other media

If an image is larger than the cell it is being inserted into, the cell will automatically expand to accommodate the item. This could have the effect of distorting the rest of the cells in the table.

2 Click on the Image button on the Common panel of the Objects palette and select an item from your hard drive

Aligning items in a table

Both text and images can be aligned by using the alignment buttons on the table properties box. However, it is also possible to apply alignment settings to an entire cell. To do this:

If you specify settings for cell alignment and then use the alignment buttons on the properties box, this will override the cell alignment settings. It is best to use one method or the other within individual cells.

The default settings for cell alignment are horizontal as left and vertical as middle.

If you are using the cell alignment option to align an image, make sure the image is not selected in the cell, otherwise this function will not be available.

Using the vertical and horizontal alignment options is an excellent way to centre items within a cell, something that could not be done with the same accuracy using the alignment buttons.

1 Insert the cursor in a cell and click here to specify the horizontal alignment that you want applied to the cell

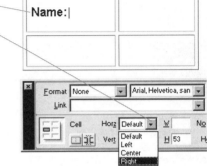

2 Click here to specify the vertical alignment that you want applied to the cell

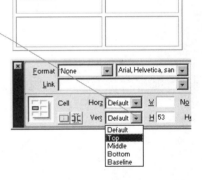

3 Any content that is then added to the cell will take on the specified alignment settings

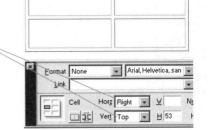

Creating nested tables

The full versatility of using tables for formatting comes when you start inserting tables within tables, or creating nested tables. This can create highly complex designs and, if all of the borders are set to 0, it can be hard for the user to tell that tables are being used at all; they just see a page with a highly sophisticated degree of formatting. To create nested tables:

When using nested tables, draw out a rough sketch for how you want your page layout to look. This should make it clearer in your own mind as to how many nested tables you want to create and where they should all be located.

1 Click here on the Common panel of the Objects palette

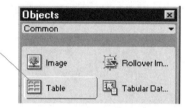

2 Specify the settings for your initial table. Select OK

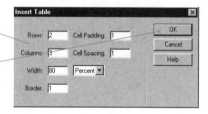

Merge cells within nested tables to give even greater versatility to your design.

3 Insert the cursor in the cell into which you want to insert the next table. Repeat steps 1 and 2

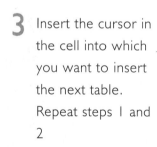

Preset designs can be applied to any table by selecting Commands> Format Table from the menu bar and selecting one of the available designs.

4 Create as many nested tables as required and then start adding content to your design

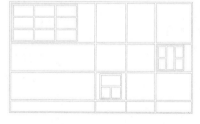

Layout view

Despite their versatility for design purposes, traditional HTML tables can sometimes be difficult to format exactly as you want them. This has been an occasional problem with Dreamweaver in the past. However, this has been solved in admirable fashion with the inclusion of the innovative Layout view in Dreamweaver 4. This is a design view specifically for creating table formats and it offers a lot more flexibility in terms of design and layout than standard HTML table creation. Complex designs can be created in Layout view and these can then be placed in the Design view, where content can be added.

Content can be added to the table layout in Layout view, as well as in Design view.

Accessing Layout view

To return to Design view from Layout view, click on this button on the Object palette:

| 1 | Click here on the Objects palette

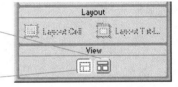

| 2 | A dialog box appears with an overview of Layout view. Click here if you do not want it to appear again

Layout view can be accessed from all panels of the Objects palette.

| 3 | Layout view looks the same as Design view, until tables and cells are created. The way to tell if you are in Layout view is whether these buttons are active or greyed out

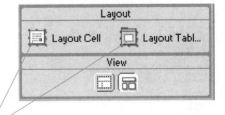

Creating cells and tables

Tables can be created in Layout view and then have cells added into them, or cells can be drawn directly into Layout view, without first creating a table. If this is done, the table is automatically included to contain the cells. To create tables and cells in Layout view:

Layout view is an excellent way to create asymmetrical table layouts. You can draw cells anywhere you like within a table, and Layout view will automatically format the rest of the table accordingly.

1 Click here on the Objects palette to create a new table

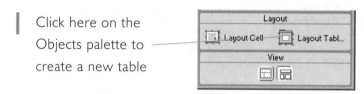

2 Click and drag in Layout view to create the border of the table.

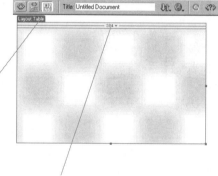

To add multiple cells without having to re-select the Layout Cell button each time, hold down Shift when the Layout Cell button is first selected. Keep it held down while you draw the cells within the table.

3 A tag at the top indicates that it is a table and its width (in pixels) is displayed along the top border of the table

4 Click here on the Objects palette to add cells within the table. (This step can be done first, in which case a table will automatically be created to enclose the cells)

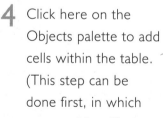

Once the Layout Cell button has been selected, cells can be created in the table by dragging within it.

...cont'd

Content and borders

If a table is created in Layout view and it has no content or table borders then nothing will be visible when it is viewed in a browser. If a border is added then the cells that have been drawn in Layout view will be visible when viewed in a browser.

Table borders can only be added in Design view. For a table that has been created in Layout view, the borders will appear around the whole table and also the cells that have been created. Although the rest of the table is outlined with a dotted line in Design view, this does not appear in the browser, unless content is added to it. If this is done, then the cell into which the new content has been added it also visible in the browser and it will also now appear in Layout view.

An entire table can be selected in Layout view by clicking once on its outer border. It can then be resized by dragging the resizing handles.

Tables that have been created in Layout view can still be formatted in Design view, in the same way as a table created in Design view. Content can be added in either view.

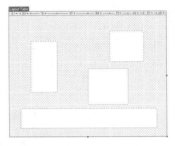

A table in Layout view, with no content or border

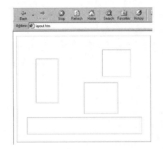

The same table, with a border, viewed in a browser

Formatting

Cells in Layout view can be moved by clicking and dragging and resized by selecting them and dragging the resizing handles, in the same way as images are resized. In addition there is also a Properties Inspector that can be used to set the width of tables and cells in Layout view and also set the cell spacing and padding and the background colour. This is accessible whenever the table is selected in Layout view.

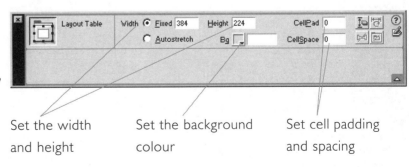

Set the width and height

Set the background colour

Set cell padding and spacing

Only one column in a table in Layout view can be set to autostretch. This can be used if you want one part of your page to remain static (perhaps the index column) while the other is stretched to fit the browser window (perhaps the main content of a page).

Even if columns are set to a fixed width, they will expand if content is added larger than the column width.

Spacer images are tiny transparent images that Layout view inserts to make autostretch work properly. They are needed to make the column think that there is content in it, even though it is invisible. Spacer images are important because, without them, cells without any content would collapse.

An autostretch column in Layout view is denoted by a wavy line at the top. Any table column can be allotted as autostretch. This means it will resize to enable the whole table to fit the browser window.

Column width

One of the traditional problems with tables is that the designer does not always know how they will appear in different browsers. Layout view attempts to overcome this by enabling different parts of a table to be given different attributes as far as its width is concerned. The options are either to have a fixed width, which remains the same in every browser, or have an autostretch width. This means that a column with autostretch will expand to fit the remainder of the browser window. By default, all columns are a fixed width. To create autostretch columns:

1 Click here and select Make Column Autostretch

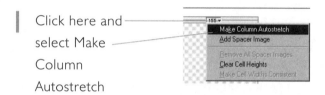

2 Select Create a spacer image file, when prompted. Select OK

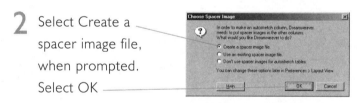

3 Save the spacer image into your Web site folder

4 The column is now stretched so that the table fills the whole screen

Frames and layers

Two of the more complex elements of Web authoring are frames and layers. Frames enable different documents to be viewed simultaneously and layers enable elements on a page to be placed on top of one another. This chapter looks at creating pages using frames and targeting links that are placed in frames pages. It also shows how to create and manage layers.

Covers

About frames | 130

Creating frames | 131

Saving frames and framesets | 133

Frames Inspector | 135

Frame/frameset properties | 136

Resizing and deleting frames | 138

Hyperlinks in frames | 139

Targeting links | 140

Using layers | 143

Creating layers | 144

Layer properties | 145

Layers palette | 146

Creating nested layers | 147

Moving and resizing layers | 148

Chapter Nine

About frames

Frames layouts are frequently used to display an index on the page, which remains there while the rest of the content on screen changes. This way, the user always has quick access to the other main areas on the site. A similar effect can also be achieved through the use of navigation bars.

Traditionally frames have had an uneasy relationship with the Web, primarily for two reasons:

- They can cause problems for people viewing pages with older browsers such as before Internet Explorer 3 and Netscape Navigator 3, and even when viewed on more recent browsers they are not always displayed as they should be. Also, frames pages can cause problems for search engines when they are trying to catalogue pages

- They are one of the harder concepts for Web designers to master, particularly those new to this medium. Although there is no particular secret to getting to grips with frames from a design point-of-view, there are some elements about it (such as the relationship between frames and framesets and targeting links in frames) that are a bit more confusing than other aspects of Web design

Practise creating and using frames and framesets before you base a Web site on them. Some people thrive on designing in this way, while others never really take to it.

The basic concept of frames is that the content of two or more pages is displayed on screen at the same time. Each page is known as a frame and numerous frames can be displayed at the same time. Each frame acts independently of the others that are being displayed; so it is possible to scroll through the contents of one frame, while all of the others remain static. This is the great strength of a frames layout: it allows different HTML pages to be viewed simultaneously, without the need to jump from one to another through the use of hyperlinks.

Frames pages are just normal HTML documents. They can be displayed as single pages on their own and they only become part of a frames layout when they are inserted into a frameset.

The final part of the frames equation is the frameset. This is the document that contains all of the frames that are being viewed. So if there are two frames on a page, this involves three documents: the two frames pages and the frameset. The frameset is a separate HTML document that has no visible content of its own. Instead it contains a command for the browser to display the frames that it specifies. It can also contain other details of how to display the frames. Frames pages cannot be displayed in a frames format without a frameset.

Creating frames

Before a frameset can be saved, the individual frames have to be created. This can be done by opening new documents and making them into frames, using preset designs, or using an existing document and adding frames to it. In all cases this is the basis for a frameset, but all of the elements have to be saved before this can be created.

Frames from new documents

Depending on how well you can visualise frames and framesets, it can be easier to build them up from scratch, rather than trying to convert existing documents into this style. However, as you become more familiar with this concept, you may find that both ways are just as easy.

1 Select File > New from the menu bar

2 Select Insert > Frames from the menu bar and select an option for how you want your frames to be created

OR

A frameset cannot be used until all of the documents have been saved i.e. all of the files that are going to make up the frames and also the frameset itself, which has to be saved as an individual document.

Select Modify > Frameset and the required option from the menu bar

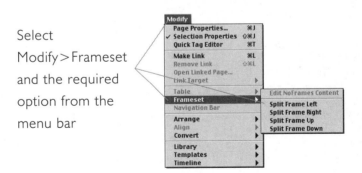

3 Add content for each frame

This is frame one   and this is frame two

Using preset designs

The preset designs can be edited after they have been selected and created on the page.

1 Click here in the Objects palette and select Frames

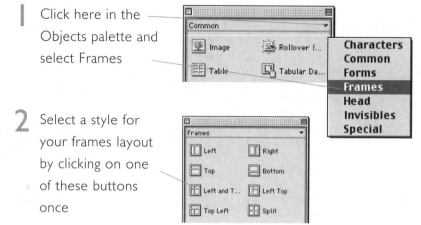

2 Select a style for your frames layout by clicking on one of these buttons once

3 The selected style opens in the document window

Existing documents can also be inserted directly into a frame structure. To do this, select a frame on screen by clicking on it once. Then select File> Open in Frame and select the document that you want to serve as that particular frame.

Converting existing documents into frames

1 Open the document you want to use as a frame

2 Select Insert>Frames from the menu bar and select an option for how you want your frames to be created

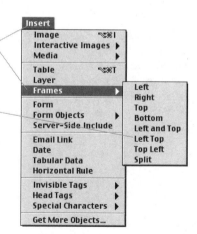

3 Or select Modify>Frameset and the required option from the menu bar

Saving frames and framesets

Once a frames structure has been created and the content for each frame has been added, the frameset can then be created. This consists of saving all of the individual frames documents and then creating a new document that will serve as the frameset. This can be done in two ways:

Saving individual items

Each frame can be saved individually and the frameset can be created at the end. To do this:

Think of the frameset as the control file that specifies which files are going to be displayed on the page and how they are going to be formatted.

1 Select a frame document by clicking once in its window

> This is frame one | and this is frame two

Once all of the frames files have been saved, the File> Save Frameset command can be activated while any of the frames are selected i.e. it does not matter where the cursor is currently inserted.

2 Select File > Save from the menu bar and name and save the file as you would with any other HTML document

File	
New	⌘N
New from Template...	
Open...	⌘O
Open in Frame...	⇧⌘O
Close	⌘W
Save	⌘S

Framesets can be named in the same way as any other HTML document i.e. 'accounts.htm'. However, in order to identify it as being a frameset document you might want to give it a name such as 'acountsframe.htm'.

3 Once all of the individual frames files have been saved, select File > Save Frameset from the menu bar. Once this has been saved it means that when this file is viewed in a browser it will automatically display the files that have been saved in Step 2

File	
New	⌘N
New from Template...	
Open...	⌘O
Open in Frame...	⇧⌘O
Close	⌘W
Save	⌘S
Save As...	
Save as Template...	
Save Frameset	

Saving all frames

1 Once the content has been added to all of the frames, select File > Save All Frames from the menu bar

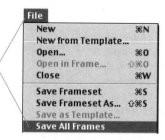

Use the Save All command to save a frameset and the files within it, if you have edited the content in the frames. Also, each individual element can be saved independently from the others. To save the frameset, select File>Save Frameset from the menu bar and to save a frame, insert the cursor in it and select File>Save from the menu bar.

2 The Save As dialog box will prompt you to save all of the unsaved frames and the frameset. The frameset is the first one. Give this a name and select Save

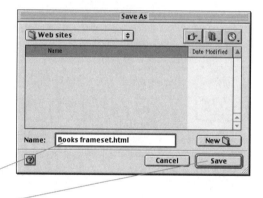

3 Name and save all of the frames in the frameset. The dialog box for each one will appear automatically after the previous one has been saved

Frames Inspector

Sometimes one of the hardest things about frames is to visualise how all of the different elements go together. This is not always obvious when they are being viewed in the document window, particularly at the stage where content has not been added to all of the frames.

Individual frames pages can be edited within the frameset or opened as separate documents and edited. Then, when they are viewed in the frameset, any changes that have been made, such as the background colour, will be visible.

To make life easier when dealing with frames, Dreamweaver provides a Frames Inspector which displays the individual frames within a frameset and also details about the frameset itself. When a frame or frameset is selected in the Frames Inspector, its details are displayed in the Frames Properties box, which is activated automatically. To view the Frames Inspector:

1 Open a frameset or create a new one. It does not matter if it contains content or not

When a frame is selected in the Frames Inspector, it is highlighted in the document window with a thin dotted line around it.

2 Select Window> Frames from the menu bar

To make a frameset structure visible in the document window, open the frameset file and select View>Frame Borders from the menu bar.

3 The frameset structure and individual frames are displayed. Click in a frame to select it and activate its properties in the frame properties dialog box. Click on the outside border to view the frameset properties

Frame/frameset properties

As with other elements in Dreamweaver, the properties of individual frames and also framesets can be viewed in the properties box and various settings can be applied. There are different properties boxes for frames and framesets.

The properties for a frames page that has been opened independently from the frameset can be displayed by clicking once on its outer border.

Frame properties

To view the properties of a frame, it has to be selected, preferably within an open frameset, but it can also be opened as an independent file.

If frames have not been given unique names they will be called Main Frame, Right Frame etc. The Main Frame is known as the parent frame in the frameset and the other frames are child frames.

The names of frames become important when it comes to targeting links in frames. For this, they can have unique names that they have been given or their default names.

1   Open a frameset, select Window > Frames and click on a frame in the Frame Inspector

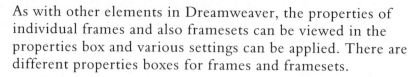

The Scroll function allows for scroll bars to be inserted if the content in the frame is greater than the available screen size. The default is for using scroll bars and this should only be turned off if you are sure that they will not be needed.

2   Click here to give the frame a unique name

3   Click here to specify whether a frame has a border and, if so, its designated colour

4   Click here to specify whether the frame can use scroll bars or not when it is viewed in a browser

5   Check this box on if you do not want the users to be able to change the size of the frame when it is viewed in a browser

Frameset properties

A frameset can be given a name by selecting it as shown in step 1 and then selecting Modify>Page Properties. Enter a name in the Title box. This is the one that will appear as the page title, rather than the filename.

1 Open a frameset, select Window> Frames and click on the outer border in the Frame Inspector

OR

Click on one of the frame borders in the document window

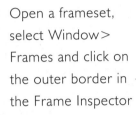

This is frame one | and this is frame two

The options for resizing frames in the Frames Properties box are:

- *Pixels. This gives the frame an absolute value that does not alter*
- *Percent. This gives the frame a percentage value of the whole frameset i.e. if you wanted two frames to take up half of a frameset, they would both be assigned a percent value of 50*
- *Relative. This gives a frame a size that is proportional to the other frames in the frameset. Pixel and Percent values take precedence over Relative ones*

2 The format of the frameset is displayed here

3 Click here to specify whether the frameset uses borders and, if so, a designated colour

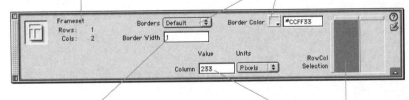

4 If borders are used, click here to specify a weight of line for them

5 Click here to specify the size of a frame, which can be determined by selecting one of the panels to the right

Resizing and deleting frames

Frames can be resized in a frameset or deleted from it altogether.

Resizing a frame

A frame can be resized by selecting the frameset and then resizing it in the frameset properties box, but it is probably quicker to resize it by dragging:

Individual frames can also be selected by Alt+click (Windows) or Option+Shift+click (Mac) within the required frames document. This activates the Frames Properties box, as long as the frames document has been selected while it is being viewed within its frameset document.

1 Make sure the Frames Inspector is showing by selecting Window>Frames from the menu bar

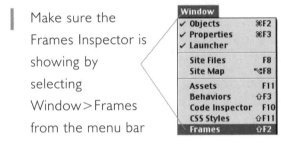

Once a frame has been resized, select the frame and select File>Save from the menu bar, or File> Select All to save all of the frames and the frameset.

2 Click on the border of a frame and drag to resize it. The Frames Inspector will display the frame being resized

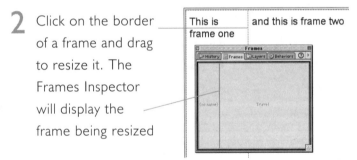

Deleting a frame

1 Display the Frames Inspector, as in Step 1 above

If a frame is nested within other frames in the document window, you may find that the frame is being resized rather than deleted when you drag it to a border on an adjoining frame. If this is the case, drag it to the opposite one.

2 Click on the border of a frame and drag it to the outer border of the frameset to delete it

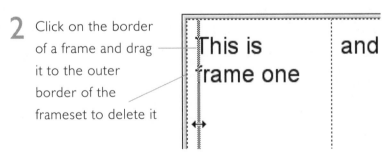

Hyperlinks in frames

Since framesets are essentially a collection of standard HTML pages displayed alongside each other, it is safe to assume that they contain exactly the same range of elements as a page being displayed on it own. This can include text, images, tables and, most importantly, hyperlinks. The reason that hyperlinks have a more significant role to play in framesets is because they do not behave exactly in the same way as on a single page. If a hyperlink is on a standard HTML page then the linked page opens in place of the one in which the link was placed. However, since a frameset has a minimum of two frames, this means that there is a choice for where a linked page is displayed. By default a linked page opens in the same frame as the link was placed:

When using hyperlinks in a frameset, bear in mind that the area in which the linked page will be opened will probably be smaller than if it were opened independently in its own window. This could have some consequences for the design and layout of the linked page.

1 In this basic frameset (created with two frames) a hyperlink has been placed in the left hand frame

This is frame one	and this is frame two
Index	

2 When the hyperlink is activated, the linked page opens up in the same frame, unless otherwise specified

Favorites History Search	This page is being served from your Mac OS computer. If you're connected to the Internet, you can make it available to everyone in your organisation, regardless of the browser or the computer they use.	and this is frame two

Targeting links

There may be occasions when you will want a linked page to open in the same frame as the one in which the link is placed. However, it is more likely that you will want to specify another frame for the linked file to open in. This is known as targeting links.

The most obvious example of targeting links is in a frameset with one frame acting as an index and the other as the main display area for the content. The links are placed in the index and when they are activated, the linked file is opened in the main frame. This means that the selected content is displayed and the index is still visible. To target a link in a frameset, it has to first be created and then you have to specify the frame in which you want it to open in the frameset:

When adding hyperlinks to a frame, make sure all of the elements of the frameset have been saved.

1 Create a hyperlink in a frame as you would on an independent page

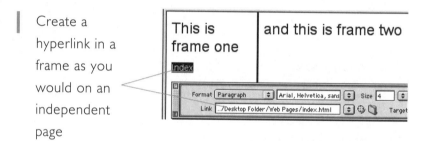

When you first start experimenting with targeting links, use a simple frameset containing two frames at first. This will enable you to get a feel for how targeting works and you can then apply it to more complex framesets. This is one of the more confusing aspects of HTML authoring so take some time to practise with it.

2 Click here in the Properties Inspector to select the options for targeting the link

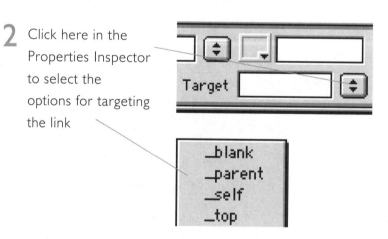

The options for targeting a link are:

Using the 'Blank' option for targeting can be confusing or irritating for users, particularly if they are not too experienced with the Web. Having more than one browser window open at the same time can make some users uncertain about which one they should be using.

- Blank. This opens the linked document in a new window and leaves the original frameset intact

- Parent. This opens the linked document in the main frame (or parent) of the frameset

- Self. This opens the linked document in the same frame as the one in which the link is located

- Top. This opens the linked document in the whole frameset, so that none of the previous content is visible

3 Once a link has been targeted, the linked document will open in the specified frame. In this example, the linked document has been targeted to open in the _self frame, which means it opens in the same frame as the link is located

The 'Top' option can be useful if you want to take the user to the start of a separate section within your Web site. This could then open as a complete window and so give more prominence to the items in that section. Also, by removing the other frames, there will be less distractions for the user.

This page is being served from your Mac OS computer. If you're connected to the Internet, you can make it available to everyone in your organisation, regardless of the browser or the computer they use.

This is frame two

4 If the targeted link had been to _top, the link would have opened as a whole page and the index would not have been visible any more

Targeting with named frames

If you are using a limited number of frames within a frameset (two or three) then it is relatively straightforward to keep track of targeting frames with the blank, parent, self and top options. However if you are using a frameset containing numerous frames, it can get confusing as to which links are going to appear in which frames.

To overcome this problem, it is possible to use frame names as the targeted links. To do this:

Frames can be named by selecting them and then entering a name for them in the Properties Inspector. See page 136 for details about assigning frame properties.

1 Give each frame a name in the Properties Inspector

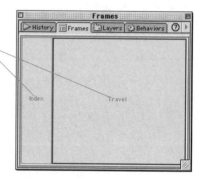

2 Add a link in a frame and click here to access the targeting options

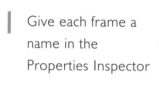

Even if frames have not been named, the target list also contains options for targeting frames such as 'Main frame' or 'Top frame' which refers to the active frames and their position in the frameset. However, this can get confusing if there are numerous frames in the frameset.

3 A list of all the named frames within the frameset will appear. Select one and this is where the linked file will be opened

Using layers

One of the drawbacks of Web pages created in HTML is that there has not always been a facility to overlap elements on a page, such as text over an image, or several images stacked on top of each other. However, Dreamweaver has made this possible with a function called layers. This allows layers of content to be added to a page, which can be positioned independently from the items that have already been included: they are placed on an invisible layer above the elements underneath, as if they were included on a piece of glass or transparent plastic.

Layers can give a degree of flexibility that has not previously been available in some Web authoring programs:

Layers are created using the <div></div> or the <span></span> HTML tags.

Both Internet Explorer 4 or later and Netscape Navigator 4 or later support the full functionality of layers. Earlier browsers may be able to display them, but not necessarily with the correct positioning.

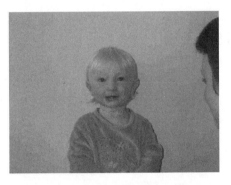

Hi this is my passport photo

Previously with Web authoring programs, it was not always possible to overlap elements on the page

If a page contains layers, always make sure you preview it in a Web browser before you publish it. This is true for all pages but particularly so for those containing layers, because the positioning can sometimes be different when viewed in a browser. If possible, view the pages with layers in different browsers.

Hi this is my passport photo

In Dreamweaver, the use of layers enables multiple items to be placed on top of each other

Creating layers

A single layer can be added to a page, or numerous ones can be included. Layers have to be inserted before content can be added to them. To do this:

Default layer properties can be specified in the Preferences dialog box by selecting Edit>Preferences from the menu bar and selecting the Layers category.

1 Click on the Layer button in the Common panel of the Objects palette

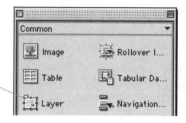

2 Click and drag in the document window to draw the layer

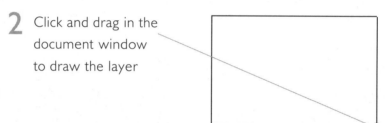

If you hold down Shift when you select the Draw Layer button you will be able to draw multiple layers on the page, one after the other, as long as you continue to keep Shift held down.

3 A layer marker will appear at the top left of the page. This is an invisible element and if you cannot see it, select View>Visual Aids>Invisible Elements from the menu bar

Layers can also be created by selecting Insert>Layer from the menu bar, or by dragging and dropping the Draw Layer button from the Common panel of the Objects palette. However, both of these methods create a layer to a preset size and, although this can be resized, it does not give as much initial control as drawing one by dragging.

4 Add content to the layer as you would on a standard page

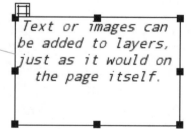

Text or images can be added to layers, just as it would on the page itself.

Layer properties

Clicking anywhere inside a layer activates it rather than selects it. This means that content can then be added to it.

Layers can be created in a CSS (Cascading Style Sheet) format or a Netscape one. CSS layers use the <div></div> and <span></span> tags and Netscape layers use <layer></layer> and <ilayer></ilayer> tags. Both Internet Explorer and Netscape Navigator browsers (version 4 and later) can display CSS layers but only Navigator can display Netscape ones.

The Layers Properties Inspector also has options for how the content is displayed (Vis) and also for inserting a background or colour.

The z-index option in the Properties Inspector can be used to change the stacking order of layers, but this is easier to do through the Layers palette (see next page)

When a layer is selected, its properties are displayed in the Properties Inspector and various settings can be applied to the selected layer. To do this:

1 Select a layer by clicking on its border once or by clicking the layer anchor point invisible element. This activates the layer Properties Inspector

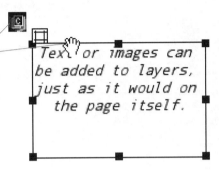

2 Click here to give the layer a name. This is advisable if you are going to be using a lot of layers

3 Enter values in the L and T boxes to specify the position of the layer from the top left corner. Enter values in the W and H boxes for the layer dimensions

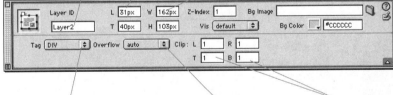

4 Click here to select the type of HTML tag that is used for layers

5 Click here to specify how the layer reacts if the content is bigger than it (CSS layers only)

6 Click here to set the visible area of layers, in pixels

Layers palette

The Layers palette can be used to perform certain editing and management tasks with layers. It is particularly effective when there are two or more layers on a page.

Accessing the layers palette

New layers cannot be created from the Layers palette. This has to be done from the menu bar (Insert>Layer) or the Draw Layer button in the Object palette.

If you do not want the content in individual layers to overlap one another, check on the Prevent Overlaps box in the Layers palette. If you then try and drag a layer over another one in the document window, you will not be able to do so.

The stacking order of layers i.e. the order in which they can be placed on top of each other, can be changed in the Layers palette by clicking on a layer and dragging it to the point you want it to appear in the stacking order. The first layer in the Layers palette is the one that is at the top of the stacking order.

1 Select Window> Layers from the menu bar

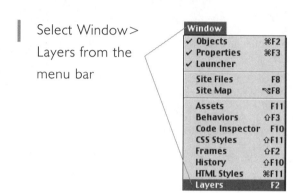

2 Click here to show or hide the layers in the current document window

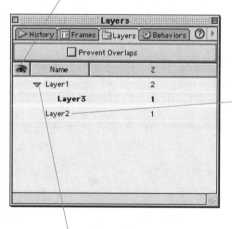

3 The earliest created layer is at the bottom of the list. Any new layers will be added at the top of the list

4 Nested layers i.e. those created or placed inside another layer are shown as being attached to the layer in which they are nested. Click on the + or - signs (Windows) or arrows (Mac) to expand or contract the nested structure

Creating nested layers

One of the most versatile features of layers is their ability to be nested inside each other. This can allow for several elements to be stacked together while remaining in the same overall layer. To create nested layers:

1 Create a layer in the document window

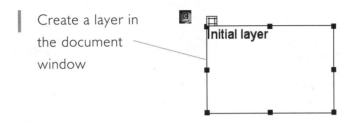

Nested layers can also be created in the Layers palette by holding down Ctrl (Windows) or Command (Mac) then clicking on and dragging a layer until it is positioned over the layer in which you want to nest it. Release it to create a nested layer.

2 Drag the Draw Layers button from the Common panel of the Objects palette and drop it into the existing layer

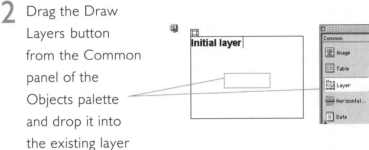

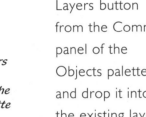

3 Alternatively, select the Draw Layers button by clicking on it once and draw a layer to the required size within the existing layer

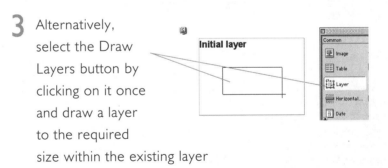

4 Alternatively, insert the cursor in the existing layer and select Insert>Layer from the menu bar

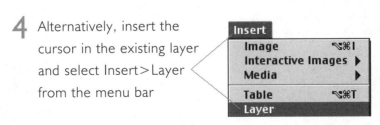

Moving and resizing layers

Layers can be moved and resized in a similar way to working with images:

Moving layers

If you insert content into a layer that is larger than the dimensions of the layer, it will expand automatically to accommodate the content.

1 Select a layer by clicking once on its border

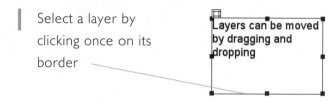

2 Click and drag on one of the borders of the layer (but not one of the black square resizing handles) and move the layer to the required location. Any content in the layer moves with it

Resizing layers

If you think your layers page will be viewed in browsers that will not support layers (Internet Explorer 3 or earlier or Netscape 3 or earlier) then you can convert layers content into a table. To do this, select the layer, then select Modify>Layout Mode>Convert Layers to Table from the menu bar. Select OK in the next dialog box. This will only work if there are no nested or overlapping layers.

1 Select a layer by clicking once on its border

2 Click and drag the resizing handles to increase or decrease the size of the layer (a layer cannot be made smaller than the size of the largest object in it)

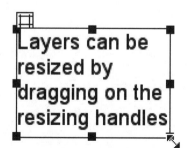

Forms

Forms enable users to interact with the author of a Web page, by answering questions and sending feedback. This chapter looks at creating forms and the elements that can be included in them.

Covers

Uses for forms | 150

Creating forms | 151

Inserting text fields | 152

Inserting checkboxes | 153

Inserting radio buttons | 154

Inserting file fields | 155

Inserting lists/menus | 156

Inserting hidden fields | 158

Inserting jump menus | 159

Inserting buttons | 160

Chapter Ten

Uses for forms

A lot of users who view Web pages like to feel that they can become actively involved with the site and be able to communicate with it in some way, rather than just passively receiving the information that it produces. The most common way of doing this is through the use of forms.

A form is a set of objects that the user can interact with to send various pieces of information to the server hosting the Web page, or directly to the author of the page. Both of these functions require a piece of computer programming called a script. This can collate the information that is collected from the form, analyse it and then send it to a specified location. This can be done with a variety of scripting language, such as Perl or JavaScript. The script can either be placed within the form itself (client-side) or on the server that will be processing the information (server-side). If it is a server-side application, this is usually handled with a Common Gateway Interface script.

Forms on Web pages can be put to a variety of uses e.g.:

If your Web site containing forms is going to be published by your Internet Service Provider (ISP), check with them first to make sure that they can process forms and also for any special requirement they need included in the form.

Common Gateway Interface (CGI) scripts are usually written in a computer language such as Perl, C or Java. This is not something that can be picked up in a couple of days and if you are not familiar with it, then leave it up to the experts.

There are a number of sites on the Web that offer information about CGIs, including some scripts that can be downloaded and used. Two sites to look at are:

- *www.cgi-resources.com/*

- *http://hoohoo.ncsa.uiuc.edu/cgi/*

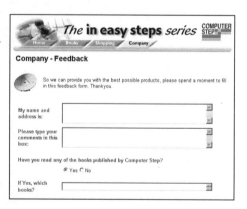

Comments forms

Questionnaires

Creating forms

A form can be made up of several different elements, all of which are contained in an overall form container. Attributes and properties can then be assigned to each element within the form structure. The form container itself can also have properties set for it. To create a form and set its properties:

1 Insert the cursor at the point where you want the form to be created

Let us know what you think

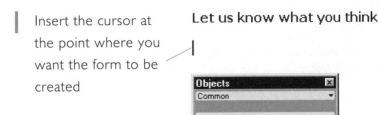

2 Click here to access the Forms panel of the Objects palette. Click here to insert a form container

3 Click on the border of the form to access its properties box

The properties that can be set for a form are:

• Name. This is a unique name that can be used when a script is interacting with data from the form

• Action. If the form is being processed by a server-side script this is selected in the Action box. Enter the URL of the script here

• Method. This is the way information is sent to the server. The options are Get, Post and Default

Inserting text fields

Text fields can be used within a form to enable users to add single line information (such as a name or address), multi-line information (such as comments or feedback) or passwords (for access to a password protected item). To insert a text field:

Text can be added in front of text fields (such as 'What is your name?') by inserting the cursor in front of the text field and typing. This is the same for all elements within a form.

1. Insert the cursor within the form container and select the Forms panel of the Objects palette and click on the Text Field button

Let us know what you think

What is your name:

Objects
Forms

Form   Text Field

When creating text fields in Dreamweaver it is possible to include text that will be visible to the user when they view the form in a browser. This could be in the form of instructions about entering text into the field. However, you should also mention about highlighting the text that is initially there and overwriting it. Otherwise your initial text will be included when the form is submitted.

2. The text field appears in the form and the Text Field Properties Inspector is activated:

What is your name: Enter name

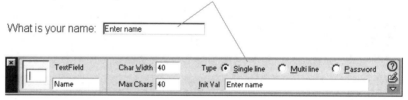

The properties that can be set for a text field are:

- Name. Every text field must have its own name

- Char Width. This is the maximum number of characters that can be displayed in the field when it is viewed by the user

The options for the type of text box are for a single line field, a multi-line field or a password field.

- Max Chars/Num lines. This sets the maximum number of characters that can be entered by the user for single line or password entries or the number of lines for a multi-line entry

- Type. This is the type of text box

Inserting checkboxes

Checkboxes can be used with a list of options that the user has to select as required. In a list of checkboxes, numerous items can be selected: it is not an either/or option. This type of element can be used for instances where you want to find out the user's preference for something like a holiday destination. To insert checkboxes:

If you want to group answers from a list, then they should all be created in the same group. To do this, make sure that the Checkbox Name is the same for all of them and that the checked value is different.

1 Insert the cursor within the form container and select the Forms panel of the Objects palette and click on the Check Box button

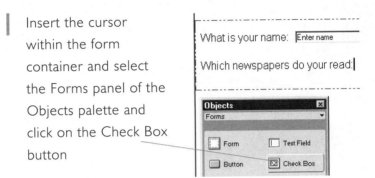

2 The checkbox appears in the form and the Checkbox Properties Inspector is activated

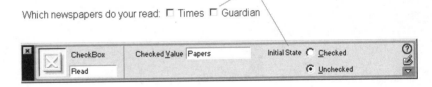

If the initial state of a checkbox is 'checked' i.e. it is selected, this could be seen as trying to influence the user into selecting this particular item. A better approach it to leave all of the checkboxes unchecked and let the user make a conscious decision to select them if they want to.

The properties that can be set for a checkbox are:

- Checkbox Name. This is the name that applies to the groups of checkboxes being created e.g. Countries

- Checked Value. This is the value that will be used in processing the form, if the checkbox is selected. Each checkbox in a group should have a different value e.g. Australia

- Initial State. This is used to specify whether the checkbox appears initially as checked or unchecked. Whichever option is chosen, the user can still change it

Inserting radio buttons

Radio buttons are similar to checkboxes, except that they only allow for a single option to be selected. This can be used for a Yes/No question or to choose one option from a list, such as, 'What is your age range', and then list the possibilities. To insert radio buttons:

Always check radio buttons, and other elements of a form, by previewing the page in a browser. This can be done by pressing F12 or selecting File>Preview in Browser. In some cases, such as if all of the required group are not given the same name, it may be possible to select more than one button. If this is the case then the properties of the buttons need to be amended.

1 Insert the cursor within the form container and select the Forms panel of the Objects palette and click on the Radio Button button

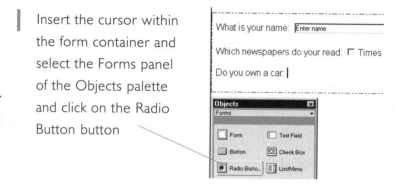

2 The radio button appears in the form and the Radio Button Properties Inspector is activated

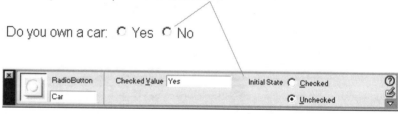

Only one radio button in a group can be selected as checked for the Initial Status.

The properties that can be set for a radio button are:

- Radio Button Name. This is the name that applies to the groups of radio button that are being created e.g. Favourite Food. Each group has to have the same name

- Checked Value. This is the value that will be used in processing the form, if the radio button is selected. Each radio button in a group should have a different value e.g. Steak

- Initial State. This is used to specify whether the radio button appears initially as checked or unchecked. Whichever option is chosen, the user can still change it

Inserting file fields

A file field in a form allows the user to select a file from their hard drive and insert it into the form, where it becomes part of the form data. This can be used if the user has a large amount of data contained in a file that they want to use in a form. To insert a file field:

1. Insert the cursor within the form container and select the Forms panel of the Objects palette and click on the File Field button

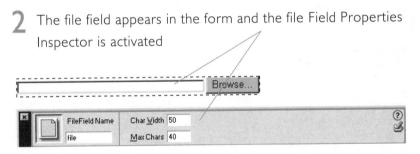

If you intend to use file fields in a form, check with your system administrator or Internet Service Provider (ISP) to make sure their server supports this function.

2. The file field appears in the form and the file Field Properties Inspector is activated

The properties that can be set for a file field are:

- FileField Name. Every file field must be given its own unique name

- Char Width. This is the maximum number of characters that can be displayed in the file field when it is viewed by the user

- Max Chars. This sets the maximum number of characters that can be used for the filename that is selected by the user

Inserting lists/menus

A list or a menu in a form can be used as a device for the user to choose from a list of items, most of which can be hidden from view until the menu or list is accessed. This is a good way to include a lot of items in a form without taking up a lot of room. To insert a list or menu:

1 Insert the cursor within the form container and select the Forms panel of the Objects palette and click on the List/ Menu button

Menus only have one item showing when the page is viewed in a browser. The other items are accessed by clicking on the down arrow that displays a drop down list. Only one item can be selected in a menu.

Lists can have several items displayed when the page is viewed and multiple items can be selected.

2 The list/menu appears in the form and the List/Menu Properties Inspector is activated:

Menu properties

- Name. Every menu must have a unique name

- Initially Selected. This is the item in the menu that appears when the page is viewed in a browser

List properties

- Name. Every list must have a unique name

- Height. This is the number of lines that are visible in the list window

- Selections. This can be checked on to allow the user to make multiple selections

- Initially Selected. This is the item in the list that is highlighted when the page is viewed in a browser

Adding list/menu items

Several items can be added to lists and menus, each with their own value. When one of these items is selected when the form is viewed in a browser, this is the value that is sent to the server for processing. Including values is the same for lists and menus:

A common use for list and menu items is for questions on forms such as 'Where in the world do you live?' The list or menu then contains all of the countries in the world and you can scroll down and select the appropriate one. This would be the value that is sent to the server.

The same effect could be achieved with a single group of radio buttons, but this would take up a prohibitively large amount of room on the page.

1 Select the List Values button in the List/Menu Properties Inspector

2 In the List Values dialog box, insert the cursor under Item Label and type the first item for the list or menu

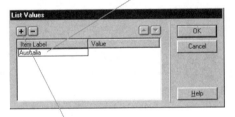

To delete an item from a list or a menu, select it in the List Values dialog box and click on the minus button.

3 Click on the plus sign to add a list or menu item and type in the name of the item

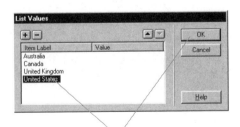

Items in the List Values dialog box can also be given values, which are sent to the server when the item is selected. If no value is used, the item label is sent instead.

4 Repeat Step 3 for all of the items to be included in the list or menu and select OK

Inserting hidden fields

Hidden fields can be inserted into a form to capture information about the user, or the form itself. Hidden fields are not visible within the form when it is published and the user does not enter anything in them. Each hidden field can contain its own value i.e. the piece of information that it will return to the server. This can include something like a name for the form (i.e. January's figures) or the date the form was published. To insert hidden fields:

Hidden fields are invisible elements and are denoted on a form by a yellow marker. If this is not visible, select View>Invisible Elements from the menu bar.

1 Insert the cursor within the form container and select the Forms panel of the Objects palette and click on the Hidden Field button

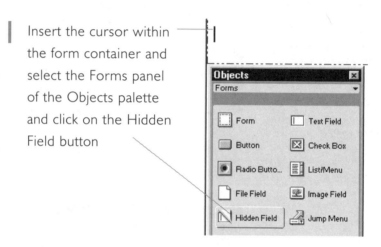

There should be no need to be secretive about including hidden fields and it could be considerate to state at the beginning of the form the information that is being gathered by hidden fields, if any.

2 The hidden field appears in the form and the Hidden Field Properties Inspector is activated

The properties that can be set for a hidden field are:

- Name. Every hidden field must have its own name

- Value. This is the information that will be sent to the server and processed as the data connected with that specific hidden field

Inserting jump menus

Jump menus are similar to lists and menus in that they provide a variety of options from a drop down list. However, the difference is that, once selected, an item in a jump menu opens a linked document or file. To insert a jump menu:

The information that is inserted into the text box serves as an instruction to the user, such as 'Click here'. It appears when the form is first accessed, but it cannot be selected.

Additionally, the Insert Jump Menu dialog box has options relating to:

- *inserting a Go button next to the menu*
- *how a linked file is opened once it has been selected*
- *a choice for including a selection prompt*

The jump menu properties are the same as those for the list/menu element of a form.

1 Insert the cursor within the form container and select the Forms panel of the Objects palette and click on the Jump Menu button

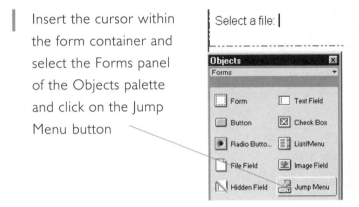

2 Enter a name for the menu item and, if required, a prompt for the user

3 Click here to select a file that will be opened when the menu item is selected

4 Click on the + button to add another menu item

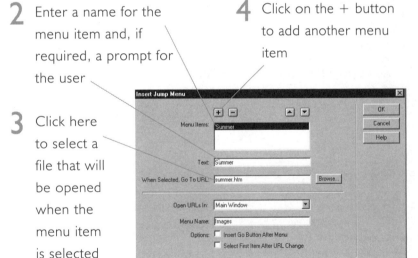

Inserting buttons

Once the user has completed a form they need to have an option for sending it somewhere. This is done through the use of a button, which is usually placed at the bottom of the form. Buttons can be used to send the information within the form, or to clear it so that it can be redone. To insert a button:

Buttons can be placed anywhere on a form, but the bottom is usually the most logical.

1 Insert the cursor within the form container and select the Forms panel of the Objects palette and click on the Button button

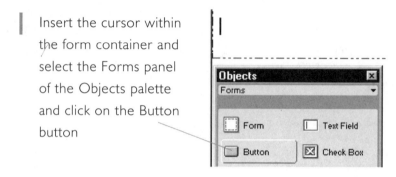

The most common wording on buttons is Submit or Reset. However, this is slightly lacking in imagination and so it is worthwhile trying to be a bit more creative, even if it is just something like, 'Send Now, Thanks', or 'Start Again?'

2 The button appears in the form and the Button Properties Inspector is activated:

There is also a form element for inserting an image field. This serves the same functions as a button, but it can be used to include an image rather than a generic button.

The properties that can be set for a button are:

- Button Name. These are most commonly Submit or Reset. By default, it is set to Submit

- Label. This is the text that appears on the button. It can be the same as the button name, or something completely different

- Action. This contains information about what happens when a button is pressed. The options are for sending the information, resetting the form so that it can be redone, or for no action to take place

Advanced features

As well as its standard Web authoring features, Dreamweaver also has a range of some of the most powerful Web design tools available, including Cascading Style Sheets, animations, Flash effects and Javascript. This chapter looks at some of these features and shows how they can be used to create high quality, professional sites.

Covers

HTML styles | 162

Cascading Style Sheets styles | 164

Creating CSS style sheets | 165

Applying CSS style sheets | 167

Animation | 168

Modifying animation paths | 170

Flash buttons and text | 171

Behaviors | 172

Javascript | 174

Chapter Eleven

HTML styles

When you are designing a Web site, consistency is important. This not only helps the user feel confident about moving around your site, in the knowledge that the layout and format will be familiar from page to page, but it also creates a professional image. Having consistently formatted text is one of the key areas in this respect and it is one that can cause problems if you try and format every piece of text manually. Unless you are painstakingly careful, you will probably miss some items that should have been formatted differently.

HTML styles are similar in their operation to those used in word processing and desktop publishing programs.

To help the designer gain a consistency with the textual elements of a site, Dreamweaver has a function called HTML styles. This lets you set predefined styles for items such as body text and headings, which can then be applied to the text within your site. This not only helps with the consistency of a site, it is also a quick way to format a lot of text. Styles can be created within the HTML Styles palette and then applied to text.

Creating HTML styles

To create new HTML styles:

The HTML Styles palette can also be accessed by clicking on the HTML Styles button in the mini-Launcher at the bottom right of the screen.

1 Click on the HTML Styles button on the Launcher palette

A new style can also be created by clicking on the right pointing arrow on the palette and selecting New.

2 The current list of styles is listed in the HTML Styles palette

3 To begin creating a new style, click the right arrow then New. Or click here

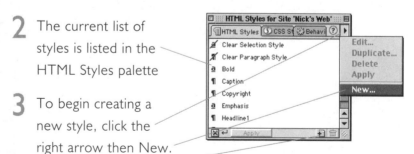

4 Double-click on the text in the Name box and give your new style a name, such as 'Sub-heading'

If a style is to be applied to a selection it will only affect text that has been highlighted. If it is to be applied to a paragraph then the cursor only has to be inserted anywhere in the required paragraph. The style will then affect the whole paragraph.

5 Check these boxes on or off to determine whether the style will be applied to a whole paragraph or just text that has been selected, and whether it will overwrite an existing style or not

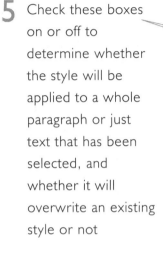

6 Select formatting attributes for the new style

7 Select OK

Styles can be deleted by selecting them in the HTML Styles palette and then clicking on the Wastebasket icon in the bottom right corner of the palette.

Applying styles
To apply a style to text:

If you want to apply a style to a whole paragraph by just clicking in the paragraph and selecting the style, then the style has to be defined as applying to a paragraph in the Define HTML Style dialog box.
If you want a style to only apply to selected text, then specify the style as a selection.

1 Select a piece of text or insert the cursor in a paragraph

2 Apply a style by clicking on it once in the HTML Styles palette

Cascading Style Sheets styles

CSS styles are only fully supported by browser versions 4.0 and above of Internet Explorer and Netscape Navigator. Earlier versions may support some CSS styles, but it is unlikely that they will support all of them.

An external CSS style sheet is a text file containing formatting attributes. It is possible to link to these and use the formatting styles with your own documents.
To do this: click on the CSS Styles button on the Launcher and click on the Open Style Sheet button in the CSS Styles palette (this is at the bottom right corner, next to the Wastebasket icon). In the Edit Style Sheet dialog box, select Link (Windows) or Import (Mac) and in the Link External Style Sheet dialog box, select Browse (Windows) or Choose (Mac) and select the CSS style sheet file that you want to link to. The attributes of the CSS style sheet will now be applied to the current document. These attributes can then be edited if required.

Cascading Style Sheets (CSS) styles are similar in some ways to HTML styles in that they are a collection of formatting attributes that can be applied to items of text or whole documents. However, they have much greater flexibility because they can also control non textual attributes such as positioning and list formatting. CSS styles can be linked to numerous files within a Web structure and when one CSS style is updated all of the affected items throughout the site are updated as well.

It is possible to link a file to an existing CSS style that has already been created, or you can create your own CSS styles within a Dreamweaver document. There are three types of CSS style that can be created within Dreamweaver:

- Make Custom Style. This can be used to create a CSS style that can be applied to selected items throughout a document, or several documents

- Redefine HTML Tag. This can be used to change the attributes of an existing HTML tag, such as a heading or a hyperlink. Once this CSS style has been defined, all of the affected elements will be changed automatically, they do not have to be selected within the documents

- Use CSS Selector. This can be used to change the attributes for specific elements within a CSS style. For instance, if you want to change the colour of a hyperlink when the cursor is placed over it, but no other attributes of it, then the Use CSS Selector can be used to edit this particular item

The code for CSS styles is placed in the head tag of an HTML page. For the Make Custom Style option, a tag is also placed around the selected text, to show that the CSS style should only be applied to this element. Once you have created a CSS style, click on the HTML Source button on the Launcher to see where the code for the CSS style has been inserted.

Creating CSS style sheets

To create CSS style sheets that can be applied to documents in Dreamweaver:

1 Click on the CSS Styles button on the Launcher

2 Click the right arrow and select New Style from the menu or click on the Add New Style button

Custom CSS styles are identified by the <class> tag in the HTML source code.

3 Click here to give the style a name and create the type here

When giving a name to a custom CSS style, it has to start with a full stop, followed by an alphabetical character. There should not be any spaces in the name. This will identify it as a '–.class' file.

4 Or click here to alter the attributes for an existing HTML tag and select the tag here

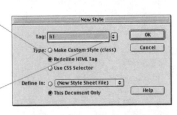

5 Or click here to select a particular attribute and select it from the Selector box

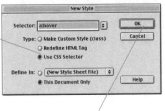

6 Click OK to access the properties for all of the above

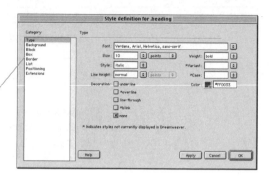

Style definition for .heading

7 Select the attributes for the CSS style you want to create. This is done in the Style Definition dialog box, which contains eight categories

The Decoration options in the Type category can be used to display hyperlinks in a format other than the standard underlined one. Check on the 'None' box under Decoration and then when this is applied to a link, it will appear without underlining.

The categories for setting the attributes for a CSS style are:

• Type. This contains font formatting attributes and also attributes that can be applied to hyperlinks

• Background. This contains attributes for background colours and images and determines whether the background is static or moves when the page scrolls

• Block. This contains attributes for aligning text and specifying how much space is placed around text

• Box. This contains attributes that can be applied to elements such as layers that are included in a CSS style. This enables you to position elements with the CSS style

CSS style formatting can be overridden by manual formatting and, in some cases, by HTML styles. If you are using CSS styles, make sure that all manual formatting and HTML styles have been removed.

• Border. This contains attributes for borders around items such as tables and images

• List. This contains attributes for formatting lists

• Positioning. This contains attributes for positioning layers

• Extensions. This contains miscellaneous attributes that are not supported by all browsers, so they are best left alone

Applying CSS style sheets

When CSS style sheets are created for Redefine HTML Tags and Use CSS Selector these are automatically placed into the head tag of the document and apply to the entire file. So, if the attributes for the H1 tag have been changed, this will alter the formatting for all of the occurrences of this tag in the document. However, with custom CSS style sheets, specific text has to be selected to have the style applied to it. To do this:

If a custom CSS style sheet is edited, all of the items that have had its attributes applied to them will automatically be updated.

1 Create a Make Custom style in the CSS Style palette and give it a name

2 Select the text to which you want to apply the style

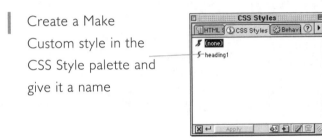

Different CSS styles can be applied within the same piece of text. To do this, select a piece of text and apply a CSS style to it. Then select a smaller piece of text within the main selection and apply another style. As long as there is no conflict between the styles they will both be applied to the smaller selection.

3 Apply the style by clicking on it once in the CSS Style palette

Bargain offers

4 The text includes details of the CSS style sheet in the HTML source code head and is enclosed by the <span> code

```
<html>
<head>
<title>Untitled Document</title>
<meta http-equiv="Content-Type" content="text/html; charse
<style type="text/css">
<!--
.heading {  font-family: "Verdana", "Arial", "Helvetica",
-->
</style>
</head>

<body bgcolor="#FFFFFF">

<span class="heading">Bargain offers</span>
</body>
</html>
```

to identify the area spanned by the CSS style

Animation

Although Dreamweaver does not have the power and versatility of a program like Flash for creating animated elements for the Web, it does offer some basic techniques for animating text and images.

Animations in Dreamweaver use the standard technique of placing an object on a timeline and then moving it between various points. The timeline is a series of frames (like the frames that make up a film or video) and you can specify what object appears in a certain frame and its position. Objects can then be manipulated in the timeline to alter elements such as their speed. In Dreamweaver, objects have to be placed in a layer before they can be inserted into a timeline to animate them. (For more on layers, see Chapter Nine). Several objects can be animated at the same time, as long as they are all placed in separate layers. To animate an object:

Flash, also from Macromedia, is the definitive program for creating Web animations. For a free 30-day trial look on Macromedia's Web site at:

• www.macromedia.com/ software/flash/download

For a detailed look at Flash, take a look at 'Flash 5 in easy steps'.

The Timeline Inspector has a frame rate for animated objects. This is measured in frames per second (fps) and a good setting for use on a Web page is between 12–15 fps.

1   Create a layer in an open document and insert an object (text or an image). Select the layer by clicking once on its border

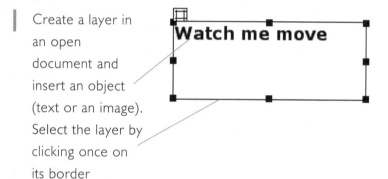

2   Select Modify> Timeline>Add Object to Timeline from the menu bar

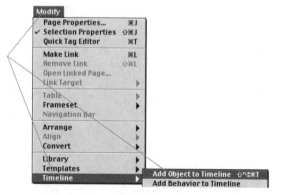

3 In the Timeline Inspector the object is positioned at frame 1 i.e. the beginning of its animation path

The bulleted dots that appear in the timeline are known as keyframes. These indicate a point where an object is positioned in a new location. When creating an animation in Dreamweaver you specify the initial position of an object in the first keyframe, select the next keyframe by clicking on it once, and then move the position of the object. Dreamweaver then creates the animation in between these two points.

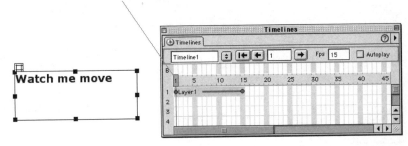

5 Move the object to a different location on the page. A line should appear — this is the path that the animation will take

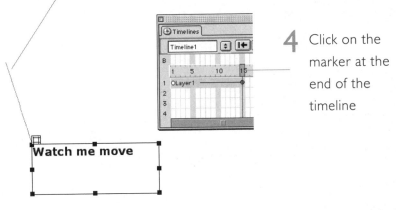

4 Click on the marker at the end of the timeline

The length of an animation can be shortened or lengthened by clicking on the second keyframe and dragging it along the timeline.

6 Drag the red marker (the Playhead) to and fro to see how the object animates

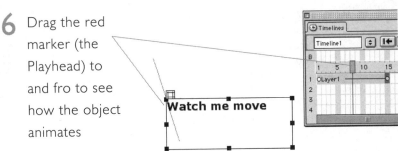

Modifying animation paths

In addition to creating straight line animations, it is also possible to create them with a curved path and also a freeform path.

Creating a curved path

1 Create a straight line animation, as on the previous page

(as on the previous page)

Several items can be animated at the same time by creating them on different layers within the Timeline Inspector (this is not the same as the layer in the document window). To do this, click on the row in the Timeline Inspector below the current animation then insert a layer and add a new object. Make sure the layer is selected, then select Modify>Timeline>Add Object to Timeline and then animate it in the same way as on pages 168-169.

2 Double-click (Windows) or Ctrl+click (Mac) at a point between the two keyframes and select Add Keyframe from the contextual menu

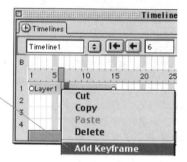

3 Move the object to create a curved path for the animation

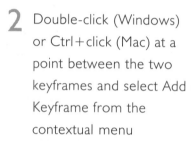

Creating a freeform path

When the Record Path of Layer is selected, the Timeline Inspector is activated automatically.

1 Create a layer with content and select Modify>Timeline> Record Path of Layer from the menu bar

2 Click and drag the layer to create as simple or complex a path as required. This is the path the animation will follow

Flash buttons and text

Flash is an animation program that has become the industry standard for producing animated effects on the Web. As with Dreamweaver, it is also produced by Macromedia and in Dreamweaver 4 some of the power of Flash has been harnessed through the use of animated buttons and text. This allows Web designers in Dreamweaver to create buttons and text that change appearance when the user moves the cursor over them. To create Flash buttons or text (the process is almost exactly the same for both; this example is for a button):

Entire Flash movies can also be imported into Dreamweaver documents. To do this, create a movie in Flash, then select the Insert Flash button on the Common Objects palette and select the required file. Select the Preview in Browser button or F12 on the keyboard to view the movie playing in the browser.

1 Select the Flash Button (or Flash Text) button on the Common Objects panel

If you are using Flash buttons or text, the users will have to have the Flash Player installed on their computer in order to view your Flash effects. It is worth putting a note on your page stating that if the Flash images cannot be viewed then it is because the Flash Player is not installed.

In some cases a prompt will appear asking the user if they want to download the Player (it only takes a few seconds) or else it can be downloaded from the Macromedia Web site at:

www.macromedia.com

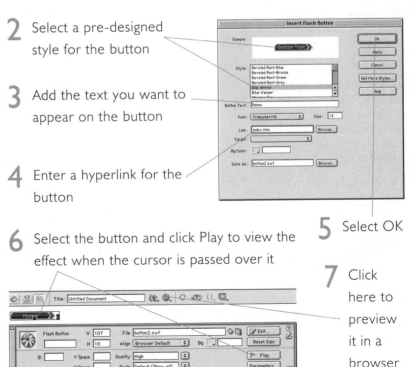

2 Select a pre-designed style for the button

3 Add the text you want to appear on the button

4 Enter a hyperlink for the button

5 Select OK

6 Select the button and click Play to view the effect when the cursor is passed over it

7 Click here to preview it in a browser

Behaviors

All browsers handle behaviors differently. Older versions, Internet Explorer 3 and earlier and Netscape Navigator 3 and earlier, have a limited range for displaying behaviors. Even versions 4 and later do not always display the behaviors as expected. In the Behaviors Inspector it is possible to specify the version of the browser for which you are creating the behavior.

Behaviors in Dreamweaver are preprogrammed events that are triggered by the user performing a certain action on the page. For instance, the action of rolling the cursor over an image could trigger the event of a sound being played. Behaviors are created by JavaScript programming but Dreamweaver contains several pre-written behaviors that can be inserted into a page using the Behaviors Inspector.

Creating a behavior consists of two parts, defining the action that is going to be performed and stating the event that will be triggered by the action. There are several events that can be selected and more can be downloaded from the Web. When an event is selected the action to trigger it is automatically included. To create a behavior:

If you want to attach a behavior to a whole page, create it without selecting anything within the document. This behavior is usually triggered when the document is opened on the Web, and is identified by the onLoad event.

1 Select an item to which you want to attach a behavior, such as an image

The script for behaviors is inserted into the head portion of the HTML source code. If you know JavaScript you can write your own scripts and include them as behaviors.

2 Select the Behaviors Inspector by clicking on the Behaviors button on the Launcher

The events associated with selected images, text or hyperlinks are usually:

* *onMouseOver, which is when the cursor is moved over the selected item*
* *onMouseOut, which is when the cursor is moved off the selected item*
* *onClick, which is when the selected item is clicked on*

A final advanced feature of Dreamweaver is its ability to include a variety of multimedia files. These can be accessed from the Common panel of the Objects palette and it usually consists of selecting the required multimedia file from the hard drive. The multimedia files that can be used in Dreamweaver are:

* *Flash*
* *Shockwave*
* *Generator*
* *Fireworks*
* *Server-side include*

3 Click here to access the Actions menu. Select the action that you want to use for the selected item

4 The action is entered and the default event is inserted i.e. the event that will trigger the action. In this example, it is 'onMouseOver' which means the action will be triggered when the cursor is rolled over the selected item

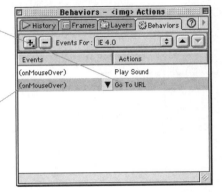

5 Click here to access alternative options from the default event, if any are available

Javascript

The Insert Script dialog box can also be accessed by selecting Insert>Invisible Tags>Scripts from the menu bar.

In Dreamweaver, some effects, such as rollover buttons, are created using a programming language called Javascript. This is a popular language for use on the Web and it can be inserted into Web pages for a variety of uses, such as producing scrolling text or dates that update themselves automatically. If you are proficient in writing Javascript, it is possible to write and insert this code yourself. (It is also possible to include other scripting languages such as VBScript). To insert Javascript into a Dreamweaver page:

Scripts can be entered while you are working in Design view or Code view, or a combination of both.

1 In the Invisibles Object panel, select the Script button

Ready made scripts can also be downloaded from the Web. There are numerous sites that offer free Javascript items for downloading. Try entering 'Javascript' into a search engine.

2 Click here to select the type of script to write

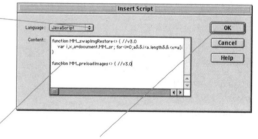

3 In the Insert Script dialog box, enter your script

4 Select OK to insert the script into Dreamweaver

5 On the toolbar, click here to debug your script in a browser

For an indepth look at Javascript and Dreamweaver, select Help> Using Dreamweaver from the menu bar and select Javascript from the Index.

6 Click here to view the functions of the script

Publishing

This chapter shows some of the checks that can be made before a Web site is published on the Internet or on an internal network. It also explains the publishing process itself and shows how to work with files once a site has been published.

Covers

Site window preferences | 176

Site management | 177

Using the site map | 178

Uploading a site | 180

Getting and putting files | 183

Checking files in and out | 184

Synchronising files | 186

Chapter Twelve

Site window preferences

When you have finished designing your Web site, you can start thinking about uploading your work onto the Web, for the world to see. This involves copying all of the files from your local Web site, stored on your computer, to a remote site, held on a server that is linked to the Web. This is usually done by a process called File Transfer Protocol (FTP) which is a protocol that enables files to be downloaded from one computer to another. Before this process takes place there are some preferences that can be set and also some site management tasks that can be undertaken. The FTP preferences apply to the site window and they can be set as follows:

If you are working on an intranet site, which operates on an internal network, then your IT systems administrator will be able to give you advice about how to upload your site to the network server.

| Select Edit>
Preferences from the
menu bar (either in the
site window or the
document window)

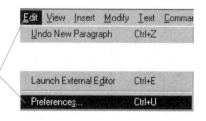

4 Click here to select how shared files are handled

3 Click here to set the location of the local and remote files in the site window

If several people are working on the same Web site, then it is possible to 'Check out' files to show that they are working on them.

2 In the Preferences dialog box, select the Site category

5 Click here to select connection and security options

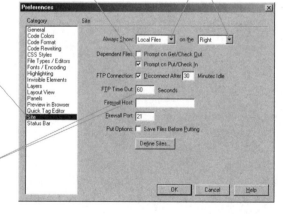

Site management

The final step before publishing a site is to check it thoroughly to make sure that everything is working properly. This involves making sure all of the links work and that everything looks the way it should. One way to do this is to preview the site in a browser and go through all of the pages. This can be done by pressing F12 or selecting File>Preview in Browser. Another option is to check all of the hyperlinks in the site window. This will generate a list of all of the broken links in your site and you can then take remedial action. To check the links in your entire site:

The Check Links Sitewide command also reveals files that are orphaned, i.e. ones which do not have any links going to them from other pages. This means that they will not be able to be accessed from anywhere else on the site. It also shows external links, i.e. ones that link to files outside the current site structure.

1 In the Site window, select the site that you want to check by clicking here

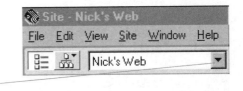

2 Select Site>Check Links Sitewide from the menu bar

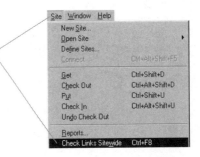

Broken links occur when the destination address of a hyperlink is changed. This can be for several reasons, such as the file's location has been changed within the site structure or the filename has been changed. If you rename or move files, try and update the relevant hyperlinks at the same time.

3 If there are any broken links in your site they will be listed in the Link Checker dialog box

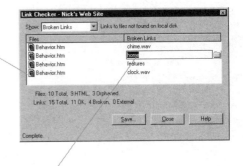

4 To mend a broken link, click on its URL and type in the correct address, or open the relevant file in the document window and select the correct link

Using the site map

The site map provides a graphical representation of a site and it can be used to perform various management tasks before the site is published.

Checking the structure

Use the site map to check the overall structure of a site. This can also be used to display broken links within a site:

1 In the site window, click here to access the site map

To open a page directly from the site window, double-click on it. It will then be opened in the document window and it can be edited there.

2 The top two levels of the site are displayed. Click on a plus sign (Windows) or the expander arrow (Mac) to see the linked files below the second level

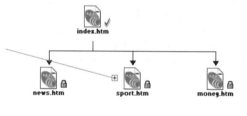

Checking in and out of files is a function that is used when more than one person is working on the same Web site. It lets everyone know who is working on a specific file. For more information on this, see page 184.

Within the site map the following symbols and notation are used:

- Red text, or a broken chain link icon, represents a broken hyperlink on the site

- Blue text with a globe icon indicates a link to a file outside the current site structure or an item such as an email link

- Green and red ticks represent files that are checked in or out

- A padlock icon represents files that are read-only (Windows) or locked (Mac)

Formatting the site map

The appearance of the site map can be customised to suit your own preferences:

1 Select Site>Define Sites from the menu bar

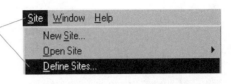

2 In the Define Sites dialog box select the required site and click on Edit

3 In the Site Definition dialog box, click on the Site Map Layout category

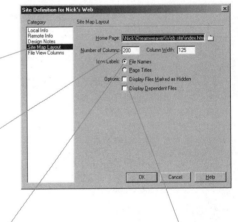

4 Enter values for how the columns of information are displayed

5 Click here to set whether files are displayed by page title or file name

6 Click here to specify whether hidden or dependent files are displayed

Uploading a site

Once you have checked your site structure and made sure that there are no broken links on a site, it is time to upload it on to the server that is going to be hosting the site. If you are working on an internal intranet, then the server will probably be part of your local network and the IT systems administrator will be able to advise you about the procedure for uploading a Web site. If your site is being hosted on the Internet by your Internet Service Provider (ISP), you will require to obtain from them the relevant settings needed when a Web site is being uploaded.

A lot of ISPs have online advice about uploading your own Web site and the settings that will be required. Try looking under their Help or Technical Support links. If possible, try to avoid telephoning, since a lot of ISPs charge premium rates for calls to their helplines. Emailing could be a useful compromise if you do not want to telephone.

The process of uploading, or publishing, a Web site in Dreamweaver consists of creating an exact copy of all of the items within your local site structure, on the remote server. This includes all of the HTML files, images and any other elements that have been included in your site. The same site structure is also retained, so that all of the links in your site will have the same location as their target destination and so work properly.

To upload a site

The local and remote structures may not always be displayed exactly the same as each other when they are uploaded, but the structures will be the same.

1 In the site window, select Site > Define Sites from the menu bar

Site	Window	Help

New Site...
Open Site
Define Sites...

When you upload a site to an FTP server, the ISP hosting the site will assign it a Web address (URL). This will probably be based on your own username.

2 In the Define Sites dialog box, select the site you want to publish and select Edit

Define Sites

Nick's Web

New...
Edit...
Duplicate...
Remove

Done

Help

The Local/ Network settings are much more straightforward than the FTP ones. Since the site will be displayed over an internal network it is just a case of specifying the directory and folder in which you want the site stored.

You will have to get the exact FTP settings from the ISP that is going to be hosting your site. In general terms the details that are needed are:

- *FTP Host. This is the name for identifying the host computer system on the Internet. It is not the same as a Web address (URL) or an email address*
- *Host Directory. This is the location on the host's server where your site will be stored*
- *Login. This is the login name you will use to access your site's files*
- *Password. This is the password that you will use to access your site's files*

Within the FTP settings there are also options for firewalls. This is a security element and you should check with your ISP first before you use these.

3 In the Site Definition dialog box, select the Remote Info category

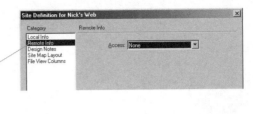

4 Click here and select FTP if the site is going to be published on the Web, or Local/ Network if it is going to be published on an internal network

5 In the FTP section of the Site Definition dialog box enter details for the FTP Host, the Host Directory, the Login and the Password. (Not all ISPs require Host Directory data, as this is assigned automatically.)

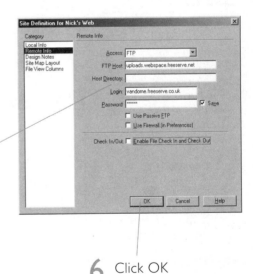

6 Click OK

7 In the Define Sites dialog box, select Done

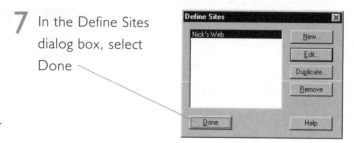

The Connect button is greyed out, i.e. not available, if the FTP settings have not been entered. However, when it becomes available this is no guarantee that the FTP settings have been entered correctly.

8 In the site window, select Connect. This will connect you to your ISP or local network

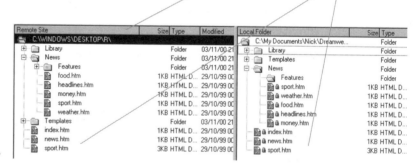

If you have a lot of images in your site structure, or a few large ones, then your site will take longer to upload to the FTP server than if they were not there. This will give you some idea of how long the user will have to wait for certain items to download when they are viewing your site.

9 If the site has been uploaded successfully, the Remote folder should be visible in the site window and contain a mirror image of the local site

If you experience problems when you try and upload a site with FTP, select Window> Site FTP log from the site window menu bar. This may give you some indication of the problem.

Getting and putting files

If you want to edit a file on your site you can either do so by opening it in the document window and then uploading to the remote site once the changes have been made, or you can open it from the remote itself and then make the changes. This involves using the Put and Get commands: Put transfers files from the local folder to the remote server and Get does the reverse:

Putting files

If a file has been edited and updated, the Put command can be used to place it on the remote server:

As with most publishing operations, you require a modem and a current Internet connection to be able to perform the Put and Get actions, if you are connecting to a remote server rather than a local network.

1 In the site window, select the file in the local folder by clicking on it once

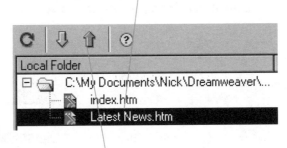

2 Select the Put button. Dreamweaver will connect to the remote network and place the file in the remote folder

Getting files

Once a connection has been made to the remote server, the connect button changes into a disconnect one. This indicates that you are online and connected to the remote server. To close the connection, click on the disconnect button. This will disconnect you from the FTP server but not necessarily your ISP connection. This will probably have to be closed down in the usual way.

1 In the site window, select the file in the remote folder by clicking on it once

2 Select the Get button to copy the file to the local folder

Checking files in and out

If you are working on a corporate Web site or an intranet it is likely that you will not be the only person working on the files that are in the site structure. If this is the case, it is important to know who is working on a certain file at a particular time. This avoids any duplication of work and ensures that the correct version of a file is uploaded to the live site.

If file checking in and out is not used, then it is possible for more than one person to be working on a file at a time, if it is in a shared environment. Unless you are the sole author of a Web site, it is recommended that file checking in and out is used.

Dreamweaver uses a system to ensure that only one person can be working on a file at a time, no matter how many other people there are in the team of Web designers. This is known as checking files in and out. For this to work properly, it has to be activated and then individuals can check files in and out as required.

Enabling checking in and out

1 In the site window, select Site>Define Sites from the menu bar

When the Enable File Check In and Check Out box is checked on, this activates another option, for adding the name that you want to use as identification for when you are checking files in and out. Make sure it is something that the rest of the design team will recognise easily.

2 In the Define Sites dialog box, select the site you want to publish and select Edit

3 In the Site Definition dialog box, select the Remote Info category and check on the Enable File Check In and Check Out box

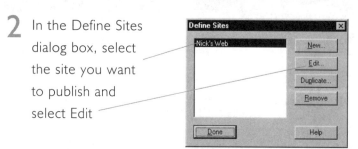

Checking files in and out

If you are working in a team of Web designers within the same site, you can check out files to prevent other people making changes to them while you are working on them. Once you have finished, you can then check them back in to make them available to the rest of the team.

When a file is checked out it is done so from the remote site. A read-only version is then placed in the local folder. The checked out version can be edited in the same way as any other Dreamweaver document.

1 In the site window, select a file in either the remote or the local folder (the one that will be checked out will be in the remote folder regardless)

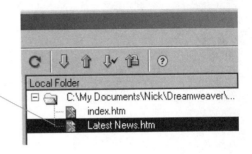

When checking files in and out, it is a good idea to talk to the rest of the design team too, just so that they know what you are doing, in case they already have some plans for the pages that you want to check out and work on.

2 Click on the Check Out button

3 You will be connected to the remote site and the selected folder will be checked out. This

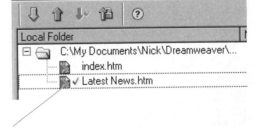

To check in a file so that other people can then work on it, select it in the remote folder and click on the Check In button. This should be done once you have finished making any editing changes and saved the file.

is denoted by a green tick for any files that you have checked out and a red one for files that other members of the design team have checked out. It is shown as being checked out in both the local and remote folders

Synchronising files

When you are updating and editing files and checking them in and out, it is easy to lose track of whether the most recent version of a file is in the local folder or on the remote site. Dreamweaver offers a solution to this problem, in the form of file synchronisation. This automatically updates both the local and remote sites so that the most recent version of all the site files is placed in each location. To synchronise files between the local and remote sites:

If you only want to synchronise certain files, select them first in the local or the remote folder and then select the Selected Local Files Only in the Synchronize box of the Synchronize Files dialog box.

1 In the site window, select Site> Synchronize from the menu bar

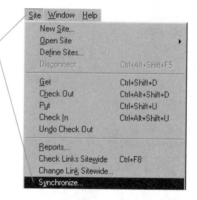

Once the synchronisation options have been selected, Dreamweaver connects to the remote site to check the versions of the files there. Therefore, make sure your modem is turned on and your Internet connection is active when you want to perform any synchronisation.

2 In the Synchronize Files dialog box, select whether you want to synchronise the entire site or only the files in the local site

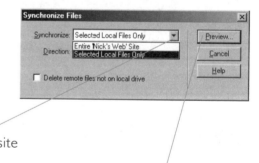

If the latest versions of all files are in both the remote and local site folders then a message will appear stating this and saying that nothing requires to be synchronised.

3 Click Preview to see the files that will be updated

Index

A

Adobe Photoshop   24
Alt tag. *See* Images: Using the Alt tag
Alternative (Alt) text. *See* Images: Using the Alt tag
Anchors. *See* Hyperlinks: Anchors
Animation   168
   Animating an object   168
   Animating with layers   170
   Frames Per Second   168
   Keyframes   169
   Lengthening   169
   Paths
      Creating   170
   Timeline Inspector   168
   Using layers   168
Assets
   Applying   61
   Favorites   60
      Creating   61
      Removing   61
   Managing   60–61
   Site   60

B

BBEdit   49
Behaviors   172–173
Bookmarks. *See* Anchors

C

Cascading Style Sheets   22, 145, 164
   Applying   167
   Browser compatibility   164
   Categories   166
   Creating   165–166
   Custom   164
   External   164
   Redefine HTML Tag   164
   Text decoration   166
   Use CSS Selector   164
CGI. *See* Common Gateway Interface
Checking in and out. *See* Publishing: Checking files in and out
Colour
   Hexadecimal value   84
Common Gateway Interface
   Scripts   150
      Downloading from the Web   150
Copy and Paste   88
CSS. *See* Cascading Style Sheets

D

Defaults fonts. *See* Text: Fonts: Default
Design Notes   40
Desktop shortcuts
   Creating   10
DHTML   42
Digital
   Cameras   92
   Photography   92
Document window   11
Dreamweaver. *See* Macromedia: Dreamweaver
Dynamic Hypertext Markup Language. *See* DHTML

E

Email links. *See* Hyperlinks: Email links
External Editors
   Accessing   25
   Specifying   24
   Uses for   24

F

File Transfer Protocol. *See* FTP
Files
   Opening 35
   Saving 34
Files and pages terminology 34
Fireworks. *See* Macromedia: Fireworks
Flash 168
   Buttons
      Creating 171
   Player 171
   Text
      Creating 171
Folder structure. *See* Structure: Folder structure
Forms
   Buttons
      Inserting 160
   Checkboxes 153
   Creating 151
   Examples 150
   File Fields
      Inserting 155
   Form container 151
   Hidden Fields
      Inserting 158
   Image fields 160
   Jump menus
      Inserting 159
   Lists/Menus
      Inserting 156–157
   Properties 151
   Radio Buttons
      Inserting 154
   Scripting languages 150
   Tables
      Inserting 151
   Text Fields 152
   Uses for 150
FPS. *See* Animation: Frames Per Second
Frames
   Creating
      From existing documents 132
      From new documents 131
      With preset designs 132
   Deleting 138
   Explained 130
   Frames Inspector 135
   Framesets
      Properties 137
      Saving 133
   Hyperlinks 139
   Inserting documents into 132
   Inspector 135
   Links
      Targeting 140–142
   Naming 142
   Properties 136–137
   Resizing 137–138
   Save All 134, 138
   Saving 133, 138
Framesets. *See* Frames
FTP 176, 180–182

G

GIFs 90
Graphical Interchange Format. *See* GIFs

H

Help 28
History palette 23
Home page
   Naming 37
   Not specified 39
   Setting
      Contextual menu 38
      From Site Definition window 37
      From the Site window 38
Homesite 49
Hotspots 111
HTML 42, 100
   Cleaning up 52
      Word HTML 53
   Comments 46
   Common tags 43
   Editors 8
   HTML Source 44
   Invalid code
      Highlighting 51
      Repairing 51
   Overview 42–43
   Page views 44
   Preferences
      Code format 47
      HTML colours 45–46
   Quick Tag editor
      Edit Tag mode 55
      Explained 54
      Insert HTML mode 54
      Preferences 57
      Wrap mode 56

Rewriting preferences   50
Roundtrip HTML   48–49
Styles   162
  Applying   163
  Creating   162
  Deleting   163
  Selecting   163
Tags   42
  Removing   58
  Selecting   58
Hyperlinks
  Absolute   102
  Anchors
    Defined   105
    Linking to   105
    Naming   105
    Top of page link   106
  Creating
    Using the contextual menu   104
    Using the menu bar   104
    Using the Properties Inspector   103
  Defined   100–102
  Deleting   104
  Document-relative   101
  Editing   104
  Email links   102
    Creating   107
  Format   100
  Frames   139
  Hotspots   111
  Image maps   111
  Navigation bars   112
  Point-to-file   108
    Anchors   110
    Document window   108
    Site window   109
  Preview in Browser   106
  Structure   101
  Uses   100
  Using images   100
HyperText Markup Language. *See* HTML

Image maps. *See* Hyperlinks: Image maps
Images
  Aligning with tables   95
  Aligning with text   95
    Experimenting   96
  As backgrounds   26, 91
  As hyperlinks   100
  Creating folders for   19
  Downloading time   91
  Effective use   91
  Image maps   93

Inserting   92
Obtaining   92
On the Web   90
Properties   93
Resizing   94
Rollovers
  Creating   97
  Defined   97
  Moderation   97
  Selecting images   98
  Testing   98
Tracing   96
Using the Alt tag   91
Watermarks
  Creating   92
Indents. *See* Text: Indenting
Internet Service Providers. *See* ISPs
Intranets   176
ISPs   16
  Form requirements   150, 155
  Uploading requirements   180

J

Javascript   150
  Adding   174
  Debugging   174
Joint Photographic Experts Group. *See* JPEGs
JPEGs   90

L

Launcher palette   11, 21
  Behaviors   22
  CSS Styles   22
  History   23
  HTML Styles   22
  Site   21
Layers. *See also* Animation: Animating with layers
  Converting to tables   148
  Creating   144
  Explained   143
  Markers   144
  Moving   148
  Nested
    Creating   147
  Palette   146
  Previewing   143
  Properties   145

Resizing   148
Stacking   146
Layout view
  Abstract tables
    Creating   126
  Accessing   125
  Autostretch   128
  Borders   127
  Cells and tables
    Creating   126
  Column width   128
  Content   127
  Formatting   127
  Spacer images   128
Library
  Accessing   71
  Explained   71
  Items
    Adding   73
    Creating   72
    Editing   74–75
Links. *See* Hyperlinks
Lists. *See* Text: Lists

Navigation bars
  Creating   76, 112
Nested layers. *See* Layers: Nested
Nested tables. *See* Tables: Nested
Netscape
  Navigator   28, 130
NotePad   24, 48

Macromedia
  Dreamweaver   8
    Defined   8
    First view   11
    Free trial   9
    Help   28
    Installing   10
    Obtaining   9
    Registering   28
    Windows system requirements   10
  Fireworks   24, 90
Macromedia Flash. *See* Flash
Menus
  Keyboard shortcuts   27
  Using   27
Microsoft
  Internet Explorer   28, 130
Multimedia
  Inserting   173

Objects palette   11
  Characters   16
  Common   14–15
  Forms   16
  Frames   17
  Head   17
  Invisibles   18
Opening files
  From the Document window   35
  From the Site window   35
  Multiple   35
O'Reilly Reference   28

Page Properties
  Setting   26
Paste as HTML. *See* Text: Paste as HTML
Perl   150
Photoshop. *See* Adobe Photoshop
PNGs   90
Point-to-file. *See* Hyperlinks: Point-to-file
Portable Network Group. *See* PNGs
Preferences   12
  Objects palette   13
  Panels   12
  Status Bar   13
Privacy statement   107
Properties Inspector   11, 19

Frame properties   20
Image properties   19
Table properties   20
Text properties   19
Publishing
    Connecting   182
    Details for ISPs   180
    Disconnecting   183
    Files
        Checking in/out   184–185
        Getting   183
        Putting   183
        Synchronizing   186
    Remote folder   182
    Uploading a site   180–182
    Web Server Info   181

Q

Quick Tag editor. *See* HTML: Quick Tag editor

R

Rollovers. *See* Images: Rollovers
Root folders   31
Roundtrip HTML. *See* HTML: Roundtrip HTML

S

Saving
    After initial save   34
    Files   34
    Save and Save As   34
Scanners   92
Scripting languages
    Adding   174
Servers   32
SimpleText   24, 48
Site Definition   31
    Window   37
Site management   177
    Broken links   177

Check Links Sitewide   177
    Mending broken links   177
Site map
    Defined   39
    Viewing   39
Site maps   178
    Adding and linking files   179
    Checking site structure   178
    Formatting   179
    Notation   178
Site window   32, 36
    Preferences   176
Sites
    Adding pages
        From document window   33
        From site window   32
    Creating   31
    Defining   40
    Naming   31
    Planning   30
Spacer images. *See* Layout view: Spacer images
Structure
    Folder structure   30
    Preparing   30
Synchronizing files. *See* Publishing: Files: Synchronizing

T

Tables
    Background images   118
    Borders
        Making invisible   114
        Resizing   116
    Cells
        Merging   120, 124
        Padding/spacing   116
        Selecting   120
        Splitting   121
    Columns   115
        Adding/deleting   119
        Selecting   120
    Design uses   114
    Editing   117–118
    HTML structure   114
    Images/multimedia
        Adding   122
    Inserting   115–116
        In forms   151
    Items
        Aligning   123
    Naming   117
    Nested
        Creating   124
    Properties Inspector   117
    Resizing   115

Rows   115
    Adding/deleting   119
    Selecting   120
Selecting   117
Text
    Adding   122
    Wrapping   122
Templates
    Creating   63
        From an existing document   64
    Editable regions
        Creating   66
        Highlighting   68
    Editing   65
    Explained   62
    Locked regions
        Highlighting   68
    Page properties   67
    Pages
        Creating   69
        Updating   70
    Properties   67–68
Text
    Adding to tables   122
    Aligning   85
        With tables   85
    As a design tool   78
    Baseline   95
    Bold
        Applying   85
    Colour
        Adding   84
    Copy and paste   88
    Fonts
        Accessing   80
        Adding   81
        Care when selecting   81
        Default   80
        Using consistently   80
    Heading styles   83
    Highlighting   78
    Indenting   87
    Inserting   78
    Italicising   85
    Lists
        Bulleted   86
        Formatting with   86
        Nested   87
        Numbered   86
    Paste as HTML   88
    Properties   79
    Size
        Changing manually   82
    Styles
        Creating   83
        Using   83
Text Styles. *See* Text: Styles
Toolbar   27
Trace option. *See* Images: Tracing

Underlined text
    Taking care when using   43
Uniform Resource Locators. *See* URLs
URLs   98, 100

VBScript   174
Views
    Switching   36

Web browsers   28
Web pages
    Background colour   84
Web sites
    Planning/creating. *See* Sites
What You See Is What You Get   8
WYSIWYG. *See* What You See Is What You Get